ENGLISH FOR PRESENT-DAY
EXAMINATIONS

ENGLISH
FOR PRESENT-DAY
EXAMINATIONS

J. B. C. BARNARD, B.A. (Hons. London)

Head of Department of English,
British Tutorial Institutes.

AND

P. LEACH, F.C.I.S., F.I.S.A.

FIFTH EDITION

(REPRINT)

MACDONALD & EVANS

8 JOHN STREET, BEDFORD ROW, W.C. 1

1954

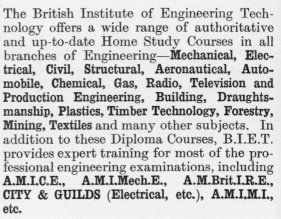

PREFACE

THIS book has been written to cover the English papers in the Examinations set by the Civil Service Commissioners, Chartered Institute of Secretaries, and other professional bodies.

It is the outcome of our failure to find a book which thoroughly covers the official syllabuses, gives due weight to the important parts of the subject, and dismisses the unimportant with sufficient brevity.

In most Examinations, especially those of the Civil Service, Essay Writing and Précis form either the whole or by far the most important part of the paper. We have, in consequence, given these branches of English pride of place, and a particularly detailed treatment. The book does not pretend to be a treatise on Grammar. Such matters as analysis of sentences, parsing, parts of speech, etc., have been excluded, first, because they find no place in most of the present-day Examinations, and secondly because, where special instruction in grammar is needed, we consider that it should form the subject of a distinct course.

The general arrangement of the book and the hints given on how to proceed and pitfalls to avoid are the outcome of many years' experience in training candidates for Examinations, and in directing and arranging their studies respectively.

We would like to take the opportunity of thanking the Manager of *The Times* and the Secretary of the Chartered

Institute of Secretaries for permission to reproduce articles and questions. We also extend our thanks to the many colleagues who have made valuable suggestions in connection with the preparation of this book.

The authors will welcome any criticisms or comments and also any suggestions as to arrangement, additions to, or improvement of the book.

J. B. C. BARNARD,
P. LEACH.

CONTENTS

SECTION I. COMPOSITION

CHAPTER I

vii

CONTENTS

SECTION II. PRÉCIS WRITING

SECTION I

COMPOSITION

CHAPTER I

ESSAY WRITING—GENERAL PRINCIPLES

THE term essay is a very elastic one—embracing at one end of the scale the brilliant essays of Macaulay and other notable essayists, and, at the other, the average schoolboy composition. Our attempt must be a considerable improvement on the schoolboy's effort, although it will doubtless fall far below the work of the classical essayists. For ordinary examination purposes an essay should be a composition expressing as well and clearly as possible the writer's thought on some subject. The groundwork of the essay—the canvas, as it were, on which the picture is to be painted—comprises accurate spelling, correct English and proper punctuation. These, however, although important, are not all. Just as colours and the skill of the artist are needed to produce a picture, so a knowledge of the subject and skill in composition are needed to produce a good essay.

Essay writing, in its highest form, is the work of genius, but the concern of the average examinee should be to ensure that he can compose an essay which will wring a little approbation from a hard-headed examiner. We shall therefore deal primarily and mainly with the principles underlying the preparation of a good straightforward essay, leaving artistic refinements, unorthodox treatment and similar literary devices to those with the natural ability to employ them.

Before passing to these principles we may usefully examine just what an essay is and what it is not. In

3

an essay it is most important for the writer to give his own ideas and feelings; not what it is usual to think, what he considers he ought to think or what he has been arbitrarily taught to think. In other words, an essay must have the mark of sincerity and individuality. In this respect Lamb—so bad a model in many ways—is admirable. No matter how singular they may be, his own ideas and no others are expressed in his essays. A good essay must be not only sincere, but also interesting. Its aim should be to entertain the reader, and examiners, who, after all, are only human, like to be interested in what they read.

Now let us see what an essay is not. Although it should entertain, it must not attempt to instruct or edify (with the possible exception of highly technical essays which need not concern us here). It should not savour of a lecture or sermon; the imperative is, as a rule, best avoided, since the reader usually resents being preached at or offered gratuitous advice.

Even more important than what we have already said is the fact that an essay must be an orderly composition, the exact opposite of Dr. Johnson's famous definition of an essay as: "A loose sally of the mind, an irregular and indigested piece, not a regular and orderly composition." The chief reason for asking an examinee to write an essay is to test his ability to express himself clearly and arrange his thoughts in an orderly manner, according to some logical plan.

Material. In examinations it is usual to give a liberal choice of subjects, and care should be taken to select the one with which you feel most conversant. Essays on technical, historical and similar subjects are probably the easiest to write *provided we have the details at our finger-tips;* if we have not, such a type of essay should be rejected in favour of a more general topic. The length of the essay must be varied according to the time allowed, but a fair average figure is 500 to 600 words per hour.

The essayist must have something to say and ensure that he says it. It is useless to write pages of trivial or irrelevant matter. There are no infallible rules for the collation of data, but some useful suggestions may be given which will help the student to enlarge his potential material, and so minimise the risk of finding himself at a loss for ideas.

The ability to tackle a subject confidently depends on the writer's mental ability and, perhaps more largely, on the information in his possession. Useful knowledge for this purpose can be acquired by anybody who leads a full and alert life, and reads reasonably widely. One's interests should be made as wide as possible, for an essay is not, primarily, the expression of academic knowledge; hobbies, sports and matters of present-day interest are quite as prominent in examination work as more recondite subjects. An interested, observant attitude towards life will help considerably in the collection of useful knowledge, but reading must remain the greatest source of information. Varied reading, not only of what is generally termed " Literature," but also on any subjects in which we may be interested, is bound to widen our knowledge; but this is not all. Of equal importance is the mental training afforded by intelligent reading. Our outlook becomes broadened and a critical faculty is developed; with increasing knowledge we begin to judge what is being read in the light of what has been read previously, and ultimately come to form our own opinions on subjects, an attainment which is invaluable both for examinations and also in everyday life.

A large mass of chaotic knowledge is not enough The habit of clear thinking must be cultivated, for this is essential to orderly expression. Meditation is not a common practice in this age of speed and hustle, but ideas cannot be clarified or sound opinions formed without thought, and a few moments spent examining and ordering our impressions is definitely not " So much time wasted."

Topical subjects are frequently set in examinations, and, therefore, an intelligent interest should be taken in current events, particularly those dealing with matters of an economic, political or sociological nature. Sound articles on these appear regularly in such papers as *The Times, Daily Telegraph* and *Manchester Guardian* and in such weeklies as the *Spectator* and *New Statesman*. In some cases, a certain bias may be shown, but it is not difficult to pick out the real facts and employ them impartially. It is a very good plan to preserve articles on matters of particular importance, in order that they may be constantly referred to.

Outline of the Essay. It is unwise to attempt to write an essay without some preliminary preparation, since, unless the writer is gifted with the somewhat rare ability to think clearly and rapidly, the resultant essay will probably be a disorderly collection of incoherent ideas. A number of steps is usually necessary to ensure that the finished article is a really good piece of work.

First of all the scope of the subject selected should be carefully considered, all ideas thereon being jotted down as they occur. Let us take the subject " Illumination." The ideas on this as they occur to us might be :

Electric, gas, candles, oil lamps, sun, stars. moon, arc lamps, filaments, incandescent mantles. Uses of lamps for miners, lighthouses and advertisements. Future developments, primitive methods of lighting, torches, benefits of electricity, convenience, cleanliness, ease of transmission.

We have here a shapeless mass of material, and the next step is to give it some semblance of form. This is done by arranging the ideas into paragraphs, each of which must contain ideas so closely related that it has unity of theme. We therefore proceed to examine the rough notes, and find that many of the ideas can be grouped together as being logically connected in theme. All the ideas, except those which are rejected as being outside our needs, should be classified in this way, so that we are left with, say, five or six groups. Each of these groups is the nucleus of a paragraph, and the ideas contained therein must be arranged in some logically progressive order.

Our material for the essay on " Illumination " could be arranged somewhat as follows :

Kinds of illuminants : candles, oil lamps, gas, incandescent mantles, electric, arc lamps, filaments.

Advantages of electricity : convenience, cleanliness, ease of transmission.

Earliest illuminants : sun, moon, stars; the savage, his fires and torches.

Special uses : lighthouses, miners' lamps, advertisements.

Future developments.

The next step is to arrange our paragraphs in some logical order so that each leads by an easy transition to the next. The train of thought must not break off too abruptly at the end of one paragraph and be taken up in quite a different place at the beginning of the next.

In dealing with the subject " Illumination," it will be best to arrange the paragraphs in roughly chronological order, thus :

The earliest illuminants.
Kinds of illuminants.
Advantages of electricity.
Special uses.
Future developments.

Characteristics of a Good Essay. The following essential characteristics of a good essay should be constantly borne in mind :

1. *Unity.* This has already been touched upon. It means briefly that each sentence must lead logically to the next one, and that each paragraph must follow on smoothly from the preceding one. In this way a really sound and interesting essay will result.

2. *Relevancy.* This means simply keeping to the point. A rather common error in this respect is to write an essay which does not fit the title. Suppose that you are asked to write an essay on " The Causes of Unemployment," it is essential to confine your remarks to the causes only. An essay on suggested remedies, however well written, will lose many marks, simply because you will have convinced the examiner of your lack of observation.

3. *Proportion.* An ordinary essay is not meant to be a complete exposition of the subject. Usually, an examinee has about an hour in which to write his essay, and the subject matter must be fitted in with the time allowed. It is a good plan to marshal the most important points and apportion the allotted time amongst them. The outstanding points should be

given most prominence, while the relatively un-important may be either ignored, or given merely passing notice.

A Typical Essay

The following essay, one of Lamb's " Popular Fallacies," is a good illustration of the points of the finished essay.

That we Should Lie Down with the Lamb

We could never quite understand the philosophy of this arrangement, or the wisdom of our ancestors in sending us for instruction to these woolly bedfellows. A sheep, when it is dark, has nothing to do but to shut his silly eyes, and sleep if he can. Man found out * long sixes.—Hail candle-light ! without disparagement to sun or moon, the kindliest luminary of the three—if we may not rather style thee their radiant deputy, mild viceroy of the moon !—We love to read, talk, sit silent, eat, drink, sleep, by candle-light. They are everybody's sun and moon. This is our peculiar and household planet.

Wanting it, what savage unsocial nights must our ancestors have spent, wintering in caves and unillumined fast-nesses ! They must have lain about and grumbled at one another in the dark. What repartees could have passed, when you must have felt about for a smile, and handled a neighbour's cheek to be sure that he understood it ? This accounts for the seriousness of the elder poetry. It has a sombre cast (try Hesiod or Ossian), derived from the tradition of those unlantern'd nights. Jokes came in with candles. We wonder how they saw to pick up a pin, if they had any. How did they sup ? what a melange of chance carving they must have made of it !—here one had got the leg of a goat, when he wanted a horse's shoulder—there another had dipt his scooped palm in a kid-skin of wild honey, when he meditated right mare's milk.

There is neither good eating nor drinking in fresco. Who, even in these civilised times, has never experienced this, when at some economic table he has commenced dining after dusk, and waited for the flavour till the lights came ?

B   * Candles weighing six to the pound.

The senses absolutely give and take reciprocally. Can you tell pork from veal in the dark ? or distinguish Sherris from pure Malaga ? Take away the candle from the smoking man ; by the glimmering of the left ashes, he knows that he is still smoking, but he knows it only by an inference; till the restored light, coming in aid of the olfactories, reveals to both senses the full aroma. Then how he redoubles his puffs ! how he burnishes !

There is absolutely no such thing as reading, but by a candle. We have tried the affectation of a book at noonday in gardens, and in sultry arbours; but it was labour thrown away. Those gay motes in the beam come about you, hovering and teasing, like many coquettes, that will have you all to their self, and are jealous of your abstractions. By the midnight taper, the writer digests his meditations. By the same light, we must approach to their perusal, if we would catch the flame, the odour.

It is a mockery, all that is reported of the influential Phoebus. No true poem ever owed its birth to the sun's light. They are abstracted works—

" Things that were born, when none but the still night,
   And his dumb candle, saw his pinching throes."

Marry, daylight—daylight might furnish the images, the crude material; but for the fine shapings, the true turning and filing (as mine author hath it), they must be content to hold their inspiration of the candle. The mild internal light, that reveals them, like fires on the domestic hearth, goes out in the sunshine. Night and silence call out the starry fancies. Milton's Morning Hymn in Paradise, we would hold a good wager, was penned at midnight; and Taylor's rich description of a sunrise smells decidedly of the taper. Even ourselves, in these our humbler lucubrations, tune our best measured cadences (Prose has her cadences) not unfrequently to the charm of the drowsier watchman, " blessing the doors "; or the wild sweeps of wind at midnight. Even now a loftier speculation than we have yet attempted courts our endeavours. We would indite something about the Solar System.—*Betty, bring the candles.*

The first quality that impresses us in this essay is its individuality and evident sincerity. We have mentioned that Lamb is a model in this respect, and this essay is typical of the manner in which he expresses his own personal feelings on the subject. Lamb was fond of late nights, and instead of uttering insincere commonplaces on the " early to bed, early to rise " theme, he says what he really feels.

This originality helps to make the essay interesting. We are surprised and delighted that the writer has the originality to protest against the usual attitude which looks upon lying down with the lamb and rising with the lark as the most virtuous and pleasant mode of life. Lamb makes no attempt to preach his views to the reader; there is nothing of the sermon about his essay.

To come down to the more commonplace features of the good essay, the unity of each paragraph should be noted. Each might be given a heading thus :

1. Pleasures of candlelight.
2. Unsocial nature of life before lights.
3. Eating, drinking and smoking without candlelight.
4. Reading best done by candlelight.
5. Candlelight the inspiration of literature.

The order should be noted; it is such that each paragraph is a natural step forward in the thought; the points are dealt with in order of ascending importance, leading up to the effective climax in the last paragraph. The arrangement preserves the continuity of thought of the essay and helps to give it unity. Moreover—a rare occurrence with Lamb—he keeps to the point; there are no digressions. Each paragraph contributes something to the central idea—the praise of the pleasures and virtues of candlelight.

Remember that although you may read the works of a good essayist with benefit, you must not attempt to imitate his style. An essay, to be worthy of the name, should reveal the author's own ideas, personality and style and not those of others, no matter how excellent they may be.

Some Pitfalls to be Avoided. The following are some common pitfalls, the avoidance of which will do much to improve your powers of essay writing.

1. Time-worn expressions such as *the eleventh hour ; like a house afire ; beside one's self.*

2. The unnecessary use of foreign phrases such as *verb sap ; quid pro quo.*

3. Verbosity, *i.e.* long, rambling phraseology.

4. Slang and abbreviations. Colloquialisms, if used at all, must be employed both carefully and sparingly.

5. Repeated use of such words as : *and, but, so, then.*

6. Humorous treatment of the subject, unless this can be undertaken both delicately and cleverly.

What to Read. The following may be usefully read with the object of increasing your knowledge of facts and developing powers of composition.

1. Political, economic and sociological matters in the daily Press.

2. Weeklies such as the *Spectator, John o' London's Weekly,* the *New Statesman,* etc.

3. Collected essays of Lamb, Hazlitt, Leigh Hunt, Addison, Steele, Walter Pater, Stevenson and Bacon. Among the more modern essayists worth studying are : Augustine Birrell, E. V. Lucas, G. K. Chesterton, Hilaire Belloc, Robert Lynd, and Arthur Machen. These are available in most public libraries.

4. As many as possible of the English classics, both prose and poetry.

5. The more provocative writings of to-day, such as the plays of Shaw, the novels and essays of Wells, Aldous Huxley, and Wyndham Lewis should stimulate the reader to think.

Notes for Essays. The following notes are given to provide practice in the development of theme, and in attaining logical sequence of ideas. Each set of notes should be expanded into a complete essay; the practice so obtained will be found well worth while. They will also show how your preliminary notes should be prepared for an original essay.

1. *The Influence of Reading Novels.* What a novel is—novels *v.* serious study—distinction between effect of good and bad books—benefits, recreation to the mind, widening of outlook on life—special attributes of novels with historical, philosophical or sociological flavour (instances of these, *e.g.* Dickens, Kingsley, Wells, Galsworthy, etc.)—necessary limitations on novel-reading—cite fiend who spends every available moment in such reading.

2. *The Use and Abuse of Advertisements.* Early advertisements—falsity caused distrust—modern tendencies—truth in advertising—proper place of advertisements, viz. the Press, hoardings, etc.—dislike of advertisements served with our entertainment as is done with certain foreign broadcasts—even advertisement films may be distasteful—income of Press from advertising—advertising by increasing demand keeps prices down—advertisement writing provides employment.

3. *The Benefits of Electricity to Industry.* Development of power, water and air to steam, and, later,

electricity—cheapness and cleanliness of electricity—infinitesimal cost where water power available for prime mover—special uses, *e.g.* electric welding, electro-magnets, conveyers, etc.—power can be transmitted over long distances—future benefits, *e.g.* when power production is centralised.

QUESTIONS

The undermentioned are topics for fairly simple essays, similar to those which frequently occur in examination papers. Each of these should be carefully considered and suitable points for inclusion in the essay jotted down and arranged in proper sequence. By doing this your powers of arrangement will be greatly strengthened.

1. The place of the cinema in modern life.
2. Rail *versus* road transport.
3. Specialisation in industry.
4. Life in a manufacturing town compared with that in a country village.
5. Describe a visit you have made to an engineering works, a museum or well-known beauty spot.
6. The uses of airplanes in peace.
7. Queen Victoria.
8. Tell the story of a burglary in which the householder is aroused but the burglars get away.
9. " Penny wise, pound foolish."
10. The beauties of Nature and the monstrosities of " art."
11. Write a letter to an acquaintance recommending a suitable place at which to spend a fortnight's holiday.
12. Trade Unions.
13. Woman's place is the home.
14. Theory *versus* practice.
15. Clothes make the man.
16. Truth is stranger than fiction.
17. If I were Dictator.
18. The joys of cycling.
19. Are we as a nation becoming lazy ?
20. Important scientific discoveries of the last hundred years.

CHAPTER II

SENTENCE CONSTRUCTION

WORDS are the primary vehicles of literary expression, but to make them intelligible they must be employed and combined in such a way that they make sense, *i.e.* into sentences, a sentence being a number of words containing a complete thought, so arranged that each sentence makes good English and is capable of conveying a sensible meaning.

An essay is an orderly collection of sentences, suitably grouped into paragraphs. Well-constructed sentences are an essential of a good essay, the sentence being the true unit of the composition. It is a fact that more essays are marred by slipshod and obscure sentences than by faulty material or bad arrangement.

Grammatical Completeness. A sentence must be grammatically correct : elementary mistakes in grammar will be heavily penalised, since it is always assumed that the writer of an essay has a working knowledge of the structure of the English language. Some of the more common errors are treated in Chapter VII.

The Simple Sentence. A complete sentence must contain a subject and a predicate. The subject is the noun or noun-equivalent about which something is said in the sentence. The predicate consists of those words describing the action performed by, or upon the subject. Thus, in the sentence " The boy is playing," *boy* is the subject and *is playing* the predicate, since this describes the action performed by the boy.

15

The essential part of the predicate is the finite verb. Finite verbs are those parts of the verb which can take a subject with which they agree in number and person. Their form is thus determined, or *made finite*, by the subject, *e.g.*

> I come; he comes; you come.
> I am; he is; you are.

Participles and infinitives are not finite verbs, and cannot take a subject; their form is fixed and cannot be limited or made finite in agreement with a noun. We cannot say : *I coming ; he to come.*

Participles and infinitives are not pure verbs, and cannot alone form the predicate of a sentence. The participle is a verbal adjective, whereas the infinitive combines the functions of a noun, adjective or adverb with that of a verb. The use of the unattached participle (see p. 96) is a common error in sentence construction.

Omission of the subject is not a frequent error, although it is occasionally found in such sentences as the following :

> With this as a background to the golden fields of corn, with a wind blowing rippling shadows along its surface, makes a beautiful picture.

Here the writer has omitted to insert the noun qualified by the phrases which are introduced by the preposition "*with.*" The sentence could be made complete by turning the verb into the passive, viz., "*With . . . . . . a beautiful picture is made.*"

A more usual error is the omission of the finite verb. This is sometimes done deliberately by a good writer to attain vigour or brevity in description. In such a passage as the following, omission of the finite verb may be justified :—

What a scene met my gaze ! Huge rollers pounding at the shore and crashing over the rocks. The wind howling like a thousand demons. The gloomy cliffs frowning amid great convulsions of Nature. And out at sea, the lights of a stricken ship tossing at the mercy of the waves.

The inexperienced writer should, however, use such a device sparingly, if at all. The careless omission of the finite verb will result in a string of notes rather than a finished composition. The following is an example of the misuse of this device :—

Often we come across skeleton hulls on the shore. All that remains of once efficient and noble ships. Valuable cargoes lost, and perhaps lives also.

Sometimes a participle is used instead of a finite verb. This error is usually, but not always, due to bad punctuation, such as the use of a full stop before the sentence is complete.

Take the passage :

The Roman and British empires were founded in different ways. The only similarity being that each reached an unrivalled pinnacle of world power.

The full stop after *ways* should be replaced by a comma.

The Complex Sentence. A complex sentence is one containing a principal clause, and one or more subordinate clauses, *e.g.*

(*a*) This is the house which we sold last week.

(*b*) Because it was snowing, he could not play golf.

In (*a*) the main clause is *this is the house*, while in (*b*) the main clause is *he could not play golf*. The rest of each sentence is the subordinate clause. The first is dependent on the noun *house* and the second on the verb *could not play.*

A subordinate clause, although it contains a finite verb and makes complete sense, cannot stand alone as a complete sentence. It must be contained in the same sentence as the word on which it is dependent. In the following, the second sentence is a subordinate clause dependent on the verb *increase* and should have been made part of the same sentence :

" Most people read in order to increase their know ledge. Because everybody has something further to learn."

The functions of the various subordinating conjunctions—those introducing clauses doing the work of an adverb, *i.e.* modifying a verb, adjective or other adverb— should be understood. Some of the more common misuses are given below.

Because is a word which should only be used to introduce a clause showing a reason for something, e.g. : *He was late because there was a thick fog.*

In such a sentence as the following the clause introduced by " *Because* " has no causal relationship whatever to the rest. *Because Leonardo da Vinci took many years to paint his picture of Mona Lisa, it is usually regarded as the greatest of all portraits.* From this it appears that the time taken in producing a work of art is the criterion of its merit, which of course is not the case.

So that is used to denote the effect of an action. For instance, we may say : " He ran so fast that he broke the record." There is, however, no sense of effect in the following : *The biscuits are packed in half-pound packets, so that in each tin there are about six pounds.*

The fact that there are about six pounds in each tin is not the effect of the biscuits being packed in half-pound packets.

Although is properly used to introduce a clause denoting a contrast to that on which it depends, e.g. : *Although he had heard of the hostile nature of the inhabitants, he determined to enter the country.* It must not be used where there is no definite contrast between the two clauses; or the result may be such an absurd sentence as, *Although he was tall, he wore no hat.*

Clarity. The usual object of writing an essay is to inform other people of our thoughts on a certain subject. It follows that clearness of expression is an essential of good composition. If the reader is left in any doubt as to our precise meaning, we have failed in the object of our writing. Every statement should be precise and definite : never vague. Much can be done in the way of attaining clarity of expression by avoiding the excessive use of such expressions as : *Perhaps ; Somewhat ; To a certain extent.* This does not mean that these terms must never be used, but only that their use should be restricted to suitable occasions.

Usually the more directly a statement is expressed the clearer will its meaning be. For instance, the following leaves absolutely no doubt in the reader's mind :

As sure as night follows day, so will I follow you. You may elude me now, but nothing is more certain than that I shall eventually run you to earth.

The whole thing is obviously a matter of conjecture, but the construction certainly leaves no room for doubt as to the meaning.

Unnecessary inversion of the usual order of words is to be avoided. The subject of a sentence generally precedes the verb, and this sequence should almost always be followed. Some writers employ an occasional unusual order of words for the sake of emphasis, but such a device is to be used very sparingly, and then only by a practised writer.

Order of Words. Ambiguity, a fault to be avoided, often arises from the careless arrangement of words, but this will not occur where the Rule of Proximity is followed. Briefly, this rule means that those words which are thought of together should be placed together in the sentence. In reading we naturally associate a word with those other words which are nearest to it, therefore if a phrase qualifying one noun is placed next to another noun, the reader will be apt to construe it with the nearest noun. For instance, in the following sentence :

There would be no objection if the economies effected were directed to the improvement of the railways only.

As the sentence stands, *only* appears to qualify *railways*, whereas it is obviously meant to qualify *improvement*. The correct order is : " *directed only to the improvement of the railways.*"

Violation of the rule of proximity may lead to such absurdities as the following :

We can hear Caruso sing years after he died by means of a gramophone record.

Caruso did not die by means of a gramophone record. The phrase *By means of a gramophone record* is intended to qualify *hear* and should be placed next to the verb : *By means of a gramophone record, we can hear Caruso sing years after he died.*

The Relative Pronoun. The misuse of this is a common offence against the rule of proximity. The antecedent of the relative must always be clear, and to ensure this the relative clause should always follow immediately after the noun it qualifies. Consider the following :

There was an interesting old building in the main street which was worthy of inspection.

From the order of the words it appears that the street was worthy of inspection, whereas actually this is meant to apply to the building. This should be reconstructed to read :

In the main street was an interesting old building which was worthy of inspection.

Sometimes the relative is used so carelessly that it has no antecedent at all, resulting in such sentences as :

The sea has its depths and shallows, of which the average is about two miles.

There is no real antecedent of " which " it should refer to a noun denoting deepness, but " depths " here has the special meaning of " deep places." This sentence could be recast as follows :

The sea has its deep and shallow places, the average depth being about two miles.

Choice of Words. The words used must express the intended meaning exactly. A large vocabulary will help greatly towards clearness of expression, and the best means of increasing our vocabulary is to read widely, especially the works of good authors. We must be particularly careful to guard against using words which, although correct in themselves, become ambiguous in their context. *e.g.*

National prosperity to which each little unit is ceaselessly working, is a case of wheels within wheels, a vicious circle.

Here there is a tendency to interpret *case* in the concrete instead of in the abstract sense. *An instance* or *an example* should be substituted for *a case*.

The vague meaning of the following should be noted :

Professional sportsmen are, as a rule, better than amateurs.

Does the writer mean by *better* more skilful, better losers, more gentlemanly or something else ?

Ambiguity. The following are some of the usual causes of ambiguity and the means of overcoming them :

1. *Omission of Essential Words.* Perspicuity must never be sacrificed to brevity, *e.g.*

Let us know if it is convenient to call to-morrow.

Who is to call, the speaker or the listener ? This should be made clear.

2. *Uncertain Use of Pronouns.* This frequently occurs where two or more of the pronouns *he, she, it, they, his, her, their* appear in the same sentence or in close proximity, the result being to leave the reader in doubt as to who or what is meant. Take the following :

The father told the son that he would have to postpone his holiday.

As the sentence stands *he* may refer to either *father* or *son*, and the *holiday* may be that of either. To make this clear the sentence must be altered to convey exactly what is meant, *e.g.* :

The father told the son that the latter would have to postpone his holiday.

3. *To avoid ambiguity it is often useful to repeat a verb, or to insert the pro-verb " do ".*

Take this sentence :—

The British do not fear the sea as much as a foreigner.

As this stands *fear* may refer either to *sea* or *foreigner*. The meaning can be made clear as follows :

The British do not fear the sea as much as a foreigner does.

4. *It is sometimes doubtful on which word in a sentence an infinitive depends :*

I took my dog for a walk to get some exercise and fresh air.

Are the exercise and fresh air for the dog or the owner ? The sentence leaves us in doubt. This could be altered to :

I took my dog for a walk in order that (*I* or *he* according to the meaning intended) might get some exercise and fresh air.

5. *The careless use of "than".* This can generally be overcome by adding or repeating a word.

" I like him better than you " should be written either as " I like him better than I like you " or " I like him better than you do."

6. *Omission of prepositions.* These should always be repeated where their omission is likely to cause confusion.

The Government cannot attend to the welfare of industry and political questions at the same time.

It appears that *political questions* is co-ordinate with *industry* with the preposition *of* understood before it.

Actually the correct preposition is. *to,* which should be inserted before *political.*

7. *The use of long and involved sentences* These should be avoided by all except the expert.

8. The judicious use of such phrases as *on the one hand* and *on the other hand* will often prevent ambiguity in the use of conjunctions.

At the outbreak of the Seven Years' War, Europe was divided into two hostile parties consisting of Britain and Prussia and Austria and France.

The perspicuity as well as the rhythm would be improved by saying :

At the . . . . . . Britain and Prussia on the one hand, and Austria and France on the other.

9. *Use of Reference words.* Such expressions as *the former, the latter,* etc., may occasionally be used to prevent ambiguity :

The Prime Minister, the President, the British Ambassador and the Secretary of State met this afternoon with the officials and experts. They received the substance of their discussions with deep satisfaction.

To whom do *they* and *their* refer ? All ambiguity would be avoided by the use of reference words. Taking *they* to refer to the Ministers and *their* to the officials and experts, the second sentence could be rewritten :

The Prime Minister and his colleagues received the substance of the discussions of the latter with deep satisfaction.

The use of such expressions, however, unless very judicious, tends to make the style of the composition awkward and stilted, and it is desirable to employ them only when perspicuity can be obtained in no other way.

Neatness of Construction. The parts of a sentence must be so closely knit together that they form a neat and compact whole. Rambling sentences whose parts are but loosely connected should be avoided :

These books, although quite clever and witty, and useful for filling in spare time on holiday, do not give any good return in the way of knowledge, not that I want to do a great deal of hard thinking on holiday, nevertheless I think it could be spent to better advantage.

The second half is so loosely connected with the first that it would be better to commence a new sentence after *knowledge*.

Sentences consisting of a long string of co-ordinate clauses joined by *and* are ugly and should not be used by the average writer. The repeated use of *so* to join clauses also results in loosely constructed sentences. It is generally better to change a *so* clause into the main clause, and the first clause into an adverbial clause of reason, *e.g.* : *There was nothing else to do so I went home* would become *As there was nothing else to do I went home.*

Rule of Priority. The last point partly illustrates the rule of priority. The principle of this rule is that unless there is some good reason against it, subordinate clauses and qualifying words should be placed before the main clause or the part of the sentence qualified. Sentences constructed according to this rule will, in addition to being neat, tend to keep the reader's interest in suspense. Moreover, the end is usually the most emphatic part of a sentence, hence greater emphasis will be given to the main statement.

Note the untidy construction of the following, due to the arrangement of the subordinate clauses :

C

The wise walker plans how many miles he will walk in one day and where he will sleep each night, before he begins his tour.

The construction would be much better if the last clause were placed first, viz., " The wise walker, before he begins . . ."

The rule is not without exceptions, as has already been mentioned, e.g. :

The visitor, who had been staying in the house for some days, when he heard of his brother's illness, departed.

The isolation of the word *departed* is bad; and also it is not clear whether the " when " clause modifies *departed* or *for some days*. Both faults could be avoided by placing *departed* between *days* and *when*. That is to say, in sentences where a main statement is qualified by a number of subsidiary ones, a strict application of the rule of priority may result in clumsiness. This can be avoided by placing the main statement in the middle, thus breaking up the series of subordinate clauses.

Where the rule of priority is observed, the sentence is periodic. Such a sentence is not grammatically complete until the last word is reached, e.g. :

With a smile on his face he entered the room.

If this is written " He entered the room with a smile on his face," the sentence could be ended after *room* and still be complete. Such sentences are termed loose sentences.

Since it observes the rule of priority, and has therefore the advantages of neatness and suspense of interest, the periodic sentence is generally preferred. If it is long, however, it is apt to get involved; moreover, a string of periods tends to become monotonous. The loose sentence is thus sometimes desirable to ensure variety, but if used carelessly it is apt to become rambling. Skilfully used, it can give subtler effects than the period. In the familiar chatty essay, where a consistently periodic style would be too formal, the loose sentence will help to give that delightful effect of a spontaneous flow of ideas typical of the true essayist.

Consistency of Sentence Structure. Where one part of a sentence balances another in thought, it is best to use the same construction for each part, so that there will be a grammatical balance corresponding to that of the thought. In the following sentence :

Where steam was used to drive machinery, now it is driven by electricity.

the change from active to passive construction destroys the balance and neatness of the sentence. It would be better to write such a sentence thus :

Where machinery was driven by steam, now it is driven by electricity.

Unity.—A sentence must deal with one main thought, and the ideas in all the clauses should be closely dependent on this main thought.

Some of the usual offences against unity are :

1. The inclusion of subordinate clauses not sufficiently closely connected with the main thought, viz. :

Being at a disadvantage, the Central Powers tried to copy the tanks, but they were unsuccessful, while the Allies pressed home their advantage by constructing the lighter and less clumsy " Whippets," and defended thus they started their task of breaking down the enemy's strong defences.

In this sentence there are three distinct thoughts : the attempt to copy the tanks; the construction of " Whippets "; the use of the tanks. It should, therefore, be broken up into three distinct sentences.

2. The misuse of conjunctions :

(a) *And.* Two co-ordinate clauses are often joined by *and*, although the statements have little connection :

Devonshire cream and cider are famous, and one of the finest towns is our destination, Exeter.

The two clauses are quite distinct in idea and should each be contained in a separate sentence.

(b) *But.* This is an adversative conjunction, and implies that there is a contrast between the two clauses joined; it must not be employed to join two unrelated clauses such as :

France is a large country but I am departing for America.

Here there is no contrast between the two clauses, which are not even remotely connected in idea.

3. A long parentheses in the middle of a sentence may tend to divert attention from the main point :

The early death of Lord Birkenhead, a most brilliant man (he won fame as a lawyer and orator, and later became Lord Chancellor and Secretary of State for India), was a great loss to the nation.

This would have been better written by making the matter in parenthesis the subject of a separate sentence.

Length of Sentences. There is no hard and fast rule as to the length of a sentence. It must depend to a large extent upon the amount of material to be included. A composition consisting entirely of short sentences would read like a child's first story-book, but, on the other hand, it may be difficult to grasp the exact meaning of a long, complex sentence because of the amount of detail which it contains.

A really good essay should consist of neither a long string of short sentences nor a few extremely lengthy ones. The ideal is a judicious intermixing of the two.

In some cases, *e.g.* where a staccato effect is desired, a series of short sentences may be employed, but remember that this is a literary device, to be used sparingly by the accomplished writer, and not at all by the indifferent one.

The following shows the misuse of short sentences :

But for a ruler to flout the law was wrong. Arbitrary rule was bad. Oppression was wrong. The motives behind these were bad.

It would be far better to combine the last three sentences thus :

Wrong, too, were arbitrary rule and oppression, for the motives behind these were bad.

QUESTIONS

(*a*) Correct or justify the following, giving reasons in each case :

1. I was very annoyed that I could not take a holiday abroad due to the fall in the pound.

2. His foible is chemistry. He has a special room for test-tubes into which he slips at odd moments

3. Alderman Smith, J.P., the retiring mayor, and his good lady have filled the mayoral chairs with dignity and decorum, rebounding with much dignity to themselves and the Borough.

4. The Prime Minister, after his hard term's work, intends to take a real busman's holiday, resting and visiting his old friends in Blank.

5. I expect to have returned next week, but I shall not do so without you agree.

6. The percentage is steadily rising, and there is no reason why it should not rise indefinitely.

7. Books must on no account be brought into the examination hall except in special cases.

8. Many goods exchange hands cheaply.

9. I met a man who climbed Mont Blanc in London.

10. No one envies you more than your friends.

(b) Convert each of the following groups of short sentences into one complex sentence :

1. The sentence on Bacon had scarcely been passed when it was mitigated. He was indeed sent to the Tower. But this was purely a form. In two days he was set at liberty. Soon after he returned to Gorhambury.

2. His fine was speedily released by the Crown. He was next summoned to present himself at Court. At length, in 1624, the rest of his punishment was remitted.

3. This was very well for a fortnight. Then one morning I received a most splendid message from the Earl of Doomsday. He said that he had read my book and was in raptures with every line of it. He impatiently longed to see the author. He had some designs which might turn out greatly to my advantage.

4. Staremberg remained master of the field. Vendôme reaped all the fruits of the battle. The Allies spiked their cannon and returned towards Arragon. But even in Arragon they found no place to rest. Vendôme was behind them. The guerilla parties were around them. They fled to Catalonia.

5. The surgeon dressed his wounds. There was no hope. The pain he suffered was most excruciating. He endured it with admirable firmness and resolution.

(c) Divide the following into simple sentences :

1. We must now change the scene to the village of Ashley, or rather to a country house in its vicinity belonging to a wealthy Israelite, with whom Isaac, his daughter and retinue had taken up their quarters; the Jews, it is well known, being as liberal in exercising the duties of hospitality and charity among their own people as they were alleged to be reluctant and churlish in extending them to those whom they termed Gentiles, and whose treatment of them certainly merited little hospitality at their hands.

2. For, as it is the nature of rags to bear a mock resemblance to finery, there being a sort of fluttering appearance in both, which is not to be distinguished at a distance, in the dark, or by short-sighted eyes, so in these junctures, it fared with Jack and his tatters, that they offered to the first view a ridiculous flaunting, which, assisting the resemblance in person and air, thwarted all his projects of separation, and left so near a similitude between them as frequently deceived the very disciples and followers of both.

3. Lastly, the devouter sisters, who looked upon all extraordinary dilatations of that member as protrusions of zeal or spiritual excrescences, were sure to honour every head they sat upon as if they had been marks of grace; but especially that of the preacher, whose ears were usually of prime magnitude; which, upon that account, he was very frequent and exact in exposing with all advantage to the people, in his rhetorical paroxysms turning sometimes to hold forth the one, and sometimes to hold forth the other; from which custom the whole operation of preaching is to this very day, among their professors, styled by the phrase of holding forth.

4. For my religion, although there be several circumstances which might persuade the world that I have none at all (as the general scandal of my profession, the natural course of my studies, the indifference of my behaviour and discourse in matters of religion, neither violently defending one, nor with that common ardour and contention opposing another), yet, in despite thereof, I dare without usurpation assume the honourable style of a Christian.

5. All authority having been concentrated in the hands of

a single minister, and the whole direction of home and foreign affairs resting with Wolsey alone, for as Chancellor he stood at the head of public justice, while his elevation to the office of Legate rendered him supreme in the Church, the check which had been imposed on the royal power by the presence of great prelates and nobles of the Council, was practically removed.

6. I remember when I was at Lilliput the complexions of those diminutive people appeared to me the fairest in the world, and talking upon this subject with a person of learning there, who was an intimate friend of mine, he said that my face appeared much fairer and smoother when he looked at me from the ground than it did upon a nearer view, when I took him upon my hand and brought him close, which he confessed was a very shocking sight.

7. Her finger being always on the public pulse, she knew exactly when she could resist the feeling of her people and when she must give way before the new sentiment of freedom which her policy had unconsciously fostered, on which occasions her defeat was given all the grace of victory by the frankness and unreserve of her surrender, which won back at once the love that her resistance had lost.

CHAPTER III

PUNCTUATION

THE meaning of a sentence is largely dependent on the position of the pauses. These are indicated by punctuation marks, and it is therefore essential to use them correctly.

Punctuation marks are thus finger-posts indicating to the reader where he should pause. They should enable him to perceive *instantly* the construction of the sentence and the positions of the pauses. Their omission or misuse often causes momentary or even permanent ambiguity. Take the following sentence :

The wind wanders sadly through the beeches and the showers of golden leaves fall to the ground.

As there is no pause indicated, the reader will probably read straight through, and before he comes to the words *fall to the ground* will take *the showers of golden leaves* as the second object of the preposition *through*. A comma after *beeches* would make the correct construction immediately obvious ; it will be clear to the reader, as soon as he reaches the comma, that the second half of the sentence is a separate clause.

There are certain rules of punctuation which the writer must observe, and we shall outline these in this chapter. It should be observed, however, that correct punctuation is largely a matter of common-sense, of noting the places where a pause naturally occurs in the reading. The nature of the stop used depends on the length of the

33

pause. Practice and careful observation of the punctuation of good writers are the surest methods of attaining proficiency.

The full stop and the comma, the longest and shortest stops respectively, are the commonest punctuation marks, and should be mastered before worrying about the less important colon and semi-colon, which are stops of intermediate length.

These are the four stops which denote a pause. The others, such as the question mark, inverted commas, and the mark of exclamation denote a special type of sentence, and their use should be easy to grasp.

Full Stop. This denotes the longest pause possible. It is inserted at the end of a complete sentence.

It is a common error to use the comma incorrectly for the full stop between sentences very closely connected: " We soon reached Canterbury, this is a very interesting cathedral city." Here the comma should be replaced by a full stop, and a new sentence begun with *This*.

There is also a tendency to insert a full stop between clauses : " I have decided, after all, to stay in England for my holidays. Whereas I had thought of going abroad." A comma should be substituted for the full stop after *holidays*.

The full stop is also used after such abbreviations as *etc.*, *i.e.*, *B.C.*

The Comma is the shortest stop, and probably the most misused. Some people are apt to insert too many commas, particularly by separating the subject from the verb by a comma, whereas in this position it is usually quite unnecessary. A comma is needed only where there is a definite pause.

The following are some of the chief uses of the comma :

1. To separate words of the same part of speech occur-

ring in the form of a list : *The road from London to Edin-burgh passes through Peterboro', York, and Newcastle. Cautiously, silently, the enemy approached.*

2. To mark off words in apposition : *Sir William Smith, the eminent lawyer, died this morning.*

3. After an absolute construction : *The king having died, the country was in confusion.*

4. After an adverbial phrase at the beginning of a sentence, and before and after such expressions as *however, moreover, of course : On the whole, the Fête was a success.*

He was, moreover, one of the most generous of men.

5. Before and after a participial phrase standing instead of an adverbial clause : *The boy, having worked hard, felt confident of success in the Examination.* Here the phrase *having worked hard* is a short way of saying *as he had worked hard.*

No commas are inserted where the participial phrase stands instead of an adjectival clause : *A clause restricting the meaning of a noun is termed an adjectival clause.* Here the phrase *restricting the meaning of a noun* stands for the adjectival clause—*which restricts the meaning of a noun.*

6. Usually between the co-ordinate clauses of a compound sentence : *I quickly reached the station, but I found that I had some time to wait there.* Where the second clause is condensed by the omission of the subject, the comma is usually omitted : *He went to bed and stayed there all day.*

7. Before and after certain subordinate clauses. Care is needed in the application of this rule, as commas are apt to be inserted in positions between clauses where they are not really necessary. As a rule, noun or adjectival clauses are not preceded or followed by a comma :

He told me that he could not come. The first Roman general who invaded Britain was Julius Cæsar. But where the adjectival clause separates the subject from the verb, or where it is itself separated from its antecedent, commas are often desirable. *Napoleon, who was a man of infinite ambition, terrorised Europe for many years.*

An adverbial clause is usually separated from the main clause by a comma : *Because we started late, we had to hurry. He went to work as usual, although he was unwell.* This rule does not always apply to adverbial clauses of effect : *He ran so fast that he won the race.*

8. Sometimes it is advisable to insert a comma between the subject and verb, where the former is very long. For example : *The committee recently formed to investigate working conditions in the northern factories, delivered its report yesterday.* The comma clearly indicates the end of the long subject. There is a tendency to use the comma much too freely, and the best rule to follow in cases of doubt is never to employ a comma unless the sense of the passage requires it.

The Semi-colon shows a pause longer than that indicated by a comma, but shorter than the full stop. Its chief uses are :

1. To mark off enumerations made by sentences or phrases, in the same way as the comma separates single words : *His talents for debate were of the first order ; his knowledge of foreign affairs was superior to that of any other living statesman ; his attachment to the Protestant succession was undoubted.*

2. To give to some clause or clauses greater emphasis than would be possible with the shorter pause denoted by a comma : *None of them was deficient in abilities ; and four of them, Pitt himself, Shelburne, Camden, and*

Townshend, were men of high intellectual eminence. Note how the long pause adds to the weight of each clause.

3. To separate sentences between which there is no definite break in idea :

'Tis a sight to enrage me, if anything can,
　To muse on the perishing pleasures of man ;
Short lived as we are, our pleasures, I see,
　Have a still shorter date ; and die sooner than we.

A new sentence is begun in the third line, but it is so closely connected in thought with the preceding one, that a semi-colon instead of a full stop is inserted at the end of the second line. Note the telling use of the semi-colon in the last line, for the purpose of emphasis.

4. To separate clauses connected by a conjunction, denoting contrast or inference : *He was told not to go ; nevertheless, he went. It was raining hard ; therefore we did not go out.*

The Colon denotes a slightly longer pause than the semi-colon ; it is often used in place of the semi-colon.

1. It is used to introduce details in explanation or amplification of the preceding sentences :

　" Alike the busy and the gay
　　But flutter through Life's little day,
　In Fortune's varying colours drest :
　　Brush'd by the hand of rough Mischance,
　Or chill'd by Age, their airy dance,
　　They leave in dust to rest."

" The following at least should be seen : the Tower of London, St. Paul's Cathedral, Westminster Abbey, the Houses of Parliament."

" For Dennis had written bad odes, bad tragedies, bad comedies : he had. moreover, a larger share than most men of those infirmities and eccentricities which excite laughter."

2. To introduce a quotation from Direct Speech, or from a book :

The schoolmaster said : " If you work hard, you will succeed."
Wordsworth spoke truly when he said : "The child is father of the man."

3. The colon separates two antithetical sentences :

The European Reformation was a religious movement : the English break with Rome was a political revenge.

The Dash is used :

1. To mark a sudden turn or digression in the sentence :

She stretch'd in vain to reach the prize—
What female heart can gold despise ?

2. To indicate suspense or hesitation :

I woke with a start—what was that noise ?
Gentlemen—er—I have great pleasure in—er—addressing you to-night.

3. After a list of words, to mark their recapitulation in the following words :

Worry, poverty, hunger—such are the fruits of failure !

4. To indicate a parenthesis :

We were all mortally afraid—I know not why—that something alarming was about to happen.

Brackets are used to indicate a parenthesis, thus performing the same function as the dash :

I consented to play bridge (a game I hate) in order not to appear unsociable.

The Hyphen is used to join the words forming a compound, such as *non-alcoholic ; anti-prohibitionist ; station-master ; man-of-war.* In Standard English it seems to be dying out, and its omission, even in the words quoted, would hardly be regarded as a serious error in punctuation. Beginners are apt to use it too freely. Only in children's spelling-books are the syllables separated by hyphens, as *ne-ver-the-less.* If, however, when you come to the end of a line, there is not room to write the complete word, it is permissible to write part on one line and part on the next, the two halves being joined by a hyphen. The word must be divided at the syllable division : thus, *mankind* may be divided into *man-kind,* but not *manki-nd.*

The Question-Mark is inserted instead of the full stop after sentences which ask questions :

Are you going out ?
Where did you find it ?

But after *indirect questions*—that is, questions reported in indirect speech—the question mark is not used :

I asked him whether he was going out.
I asked him where he found it.

The Exclamation Mark is used after interjections or sentences expressing strong feeling :

Would to Heaven that thou hadst thought right to keep it secret !
Bravo ! A fine victory.

It is also used after an apostrophe (the figure of speech, not the punctuation mark) :

Hail to thee, blithe spirit !

Inverted Commas indicate a quotation either of the words of the speaker in direct speech, or from a book :

" What are you doing ? " he said.

Inverted commas are not used where the speech is indirect or reported :

He asked what the other was doing.

They are inserted at the beginning and end of the whole passage quoted, not of each sentence, paragraph or verse. However, when long passages are quoted, an additional inverted comma is often inserted at the beginning (but not at the end) of each verse or paragraph :

" A slumber did my spirit seal;
I had no human fears :
She seem'd a thing that could not feel
The touch of earthly years.

" No motion has she now, no force ;
She neither hears nor sees ;
Roll'd round in earth's diurnal course,
With rocks, and stones, and trees."

The Apostrophe denotes the omission of a letter or letters. Its most common use is to form the genitive case, when it is inserted before the *s* in the singular but after it in the plural : *The boy's book ; The dog's kennel.* But : *The boys' books ; The dogs' kennels.*

It is also used to indicate the omission of letters in certain abbreviations : *Didn't ; Middlesbro' ; I'm.*

The apostrophe is often inserted where it is not required, before the *s* of the plural of nouns, and of possessive pronouns : *Field's, house's, your's, our's.*

In none of these examples is the apostrophe correct.

This usage, however, is correct where the words *Field's* and *House's* are taken as the genitive singular nouns, although it is better to avoid this construction by altering the arrangement of the sentence.

It is a very common error to insert an apostrophe before the *s* of the possessive adjective *its*. The form *it's* denotes not the possessive adjective, but an abbreviation for *it is*.

Capital Letters. A capital letter is used at the beginning of a sentence, and also for certain words. The chief of these are proper names : *John, Henry, England, France ;* and proper adjectives : *English, French.* Titles, when a particular individual is referred to, are begun with a capital : *King George ; the Duke of Norfolk.* But when the titles are used in a more general way, the capital letter is not used :

Some kings have been tyrants.

All the popes were not models of virtue.

Similarly with institutions :

The Church was recovering under the influence of the Counter Reformation.

The deputation was told that the Cabinet was considering the matter.

But :

We are told that fewer people go to church now than formerly.

The development of the cabinet is a remarkable feature of eighteenth-century England.

Underscoring is a useful device for drawing attention to important points. It performs the same function in writing as italics do in printing. Its use is not desirable in essay writing, but it may be employed for such purposes as note-taking, and preparation of notes for an essay, or in précis-writing.

D

QUESTIONS

Punctuate the following passages, inserting capital letters, etc., where necessary :

1. fergus paused it is an act of friendship which you should command could it be useful or lead to the righting your honour but in the present case i doubt if your commanding officer would give you the meeting on account of his having taken measures which however harsh and exasperating were still within the strict bounds of his duty besides gardiner is a precise huguenot and has adopted certain ideas about the sinfulness of such rencontres from which it would be impossible to make him depart especially as his courage is beyond all suspicion and besides i i to tell the truth i dare not at this moment for some very weighty reasons go near any of the military quarters or garrisons belonging to the government.

2. the king although he be as learned a person as any in his dominions had been educated in the study of philosophy and particularly mathematics yet when he observed my shape exactly and saw me walk erect before i began to speak conceived i might be a piece of clockwork which is in that country arrived to a very great perfection contrived by some ingenious artist.

3. it became the citizens special business to obtain from the crown or from their lords wider commercial privileges rights of coinage grants of fairs and exemption from tolls while within the town itself they framed regulations as to the sale and quality of goods the control of markets and the recovery of debts.

4. as he was doing so miss thorne who had hardly sat down for a moment came into the room and seeing him standing was greatly distressed oh my dear mr arabin said she have you never sat down yet i am so distressed you of all men too mr arabin assured her that he had only just come into the room that is the very reason why you should lose no time come ill make room for you thankee my dear she said seeing that miss bold was making an attempt to move from her chair but i would not for worlds see you stir for all

the ladies would think it necessary to follow but perhaps if mr stanhope has done just for a moment mr stanhope till i get another chair.

5. early in 1757 the prussian army in saxony began to move through four defiles in the mountains they came pouring into bohemia prague was the kings first move but the ulterior object was probably vienna at prague lay marshal brown with one great army daun the most cautious and fortunate of the austrian captains was advancing with another frederic determined to overwhelm brown before daun should arrive on the sixth day of may was fought under those walls which a hundred and thirty years before had witnessed the victory of the catholic league and the flight of the unhappy prelate a battle more bloody than any which europe saw during the long interval between malplaquet and eylau.

CHAPTER IV

THE PARAGRAPH

Construction of Paragraphs. A paragraph comprises a number of sentences all dealing with one definite theme, which gives unity to the whole. The sentences should be closely related, so that at the end of the paragraph the reader will sense a definite break. This is not to say that at the end of a paragraph the thought should abruptly break off. It must not; each paragraph must be a logical step forward from the preceding one. But at the end of a paragraph the reader should feel that a topic has been disposed of, that a link in the chain of thought has been forged.

Length of Paragraph. The length of a paragraph, like that of a sentence, is dependent on the amount of relevant matter that should be included in the paragraph. There is thus no rule as to length; the only rule is that a new paragraph must be begun when the writer has finished with one topic and is about to deal with another. A new paragraph must not be begun before this change of topic. The rule is one topic—one paragraph. To illustrate this point consider the following passages :

There are those who maintain that the warriors of old must have been infinitely more fearless and daring than the soldiers of to-day. There is no sense in making such a statement, for as the conditions under which they fought and do fight are different so it is that the types of courage required differ.

44

It requires as much courage to crouch in a miserable hole in the earth for hours, whilst immense projectiles tear up the ground all around, as to fight a man hand to hand with edged weapons. The only difference is that the type of courage required is different. The methods of modern warfare excel those of every previous age in their ability to kill off huge numbers of men, women and children, whether combatants or not. Many see in this the hand of Providence, for they contend that it is the way which Nature reserves for use when overcrowding of the population threatens. Certainly the desire to make war appears to be inherent in man, and it may be that overcrowding coincides with a vibration which throws humanity into a war fever, which will only be soothed by an orgy of killing and destruction such as took place in the Great War.

In these two paragraphs two themes are dealt with, viz., the comparison of the courage of ancient and of modern soldiers, and the effects of modern war in preventing overcrowding of the population. The paragraph division should coincide with the change of topic. Therefore, the sentence beginning : *The methods of modern warfare* should start the new paragraph. The arrangement in the passage quoted is not good, because the first two sentences of the second paragraph are simply a continuation of the theme of the first.

Although there is no rule to prevent paragraphs from being very long or very short, in practice such paragraphs have certain disadvantages. A very long paragraph presents a solid mass of type or writing which may repel the reader ; he will read with a sense of effort. On the other hand, a series of very short paragraphs, like a succession of short sentences, usually makes for a jerky.

staccato style. Again, the force of the paragraph division is weakened if it occurs after almost every sentence. Paragraphs are reduced to the level of sentences. However, it is often very effective to give a very important sentence a paragraph to itself.

Dickens, by the correct use of short paragraphs, attains a humorous effect which would otherwise be impossible. A long paragraph, properly used, may be made to convey a feeling of dignity or rhythm. The works of Gibbon and Ruskin abound in lengthy paragraphs.

Unity. The rule for beginning a new paragraph means that each paragraph must have unity of theme. It must deal with one definite topic, and all matter irrelevant to that topic must be excluded.

Offences against Unity. 1. The following paragraph consists of two sentences, dealing with quite different topics :

The first session of the League of Nations was held at Geneva, and at this meeting the forty-two nations which had joined were represented. The Locarno Treaty provided for Germany's entry into the League.

The first deals with the first session of the League, the second with Germany's entry some years later. Their juxtaposition in the same paragraph is a bad mistake.

2. An irrelevant sentence is often included at the beginning or end of paragraph :

Nothing is more inconvenient for the untidy man than getting up in the morning. Whether it is easier for a person to get up on a cold morning than on a warm one is a matter of opinion. Some say that it is easier to get up on a cold one, and I am inclined to agree with them, for on a cold morning bed is not so seductive a place, and we jump from it with greater ease.

The first sentence appears to state the theme, but the following matter, instead of expanding this, deals with quite another aspect of the subject of getting up. The first sentence is therefore irrelevant.

Position of the Theme. The theme of the paragraph must always be clear. It is usually stated in the first sentence, thereby giving prominence to the principal statement. The following sentences, like the subordinate clauses of a complex sentence, explain, expand or modify the theme, which may be likened to the principal clause of a sentence. This position of the theme has the advantage of clarity; the subject of the paragraph is immediately obvious, and the effect of the paragraph division, of the change of topic, is heightened. In the following paragraph each sentence is related to the theme stated at the beginning :

Religious persecution was unknown under his government, unless some foolish and unjust restrictions which lay upon the Jews may be regarded as forming an exception. His policy with respect to the Catholics of Silesia presented an honourable contrast to the policy which, under very similar circumstances, England long followed with respect to the Catholics of Ireland. Every form of religion and irreligion found an asylum in the State. The scoffer whom the parliaments of France had sentenced to a cruel death was consoled by a commission in the Prussian service. The Jesuit who could show his face nowhere else, who in Britain was still subject to penal laws, who was proscribed by France, Spain, Portugal and Naples, who had been given up even by the Vatican, found safety and the means of subsistence in the Prussian dominions.

The first sentence states the absence of religious persecution in Prussia, and Macaulay proceeds to give a series of examples of this.

Sometimes, it is effective to place the theme-sentence later in the paragraph, the preceding steps leading to it gradually. By this arrangement, interest is kept in suspense, and the force of the important sentence is heightened by its coming after a series of preparatory steps.

There is not always a definite sentence on which we can put our finger and say "There is the theme of the paragraph." Yet, although it is not expressed, there is a definite theme which binds the component sentences into a unity. This is particularly the case with narrative essays, where each paragraph will deal with a stage or an episode in the narrative, although this may not be actually stated. For example, the following paragraph is a complete episode :

It was the depth of winter. The cold was severe and the roads heavy with mire. But the Prussians pressed on. Resistance was impossible. The Austrian army was then neither numerous nor efficient. The small portion of that army which lay in Silesia was unprepared for hostilities. Glogau was blockaded ; Breslau opened its gates ; Ohlau was evacuated. A few scattered garrisons still held out ; but the whole open country was subjugated ; no enemy ventured to encounter the king in the field ; and before the end of January 1741 he returned to receive the congratulations of his subjects at Berlin.

The theme of this paragraph is Frederick's winter campaign of 1740–1, although it is not actually stated in any one sentence.

Logical Order of Sentences. The sentences of a paragraph must be arranged so that there is an orderly and continuous progress in the thought from the first to the last. The thought must not suddenly double back or break off. If there is a natural chronological order, this should be followed. Note the awkward way in which the narrative goes back to develop a previous statement after the second sentence, in the following :

Such were the terrors of the last war that a League of Nations was formed to prevent the outbreak of further wars. Yet already Japan and China are fighting. It was believed that the world was coming to an end. Not only in the battle-field was destruction wrought; aeroplanes carrying bombs did much damage in attempts to destroy soldiers' camps in England.

To give a logical and continuous sequence of thought to the paragraph, we should arrange it thus :

The last war was indeed terrible. It was believed that the world was coming to an end. Not only in the battle-field was destruction wrought; aeroplanes carrying bombs did much damage in attempts to destroy soldiers' camps in England. Such were its terrors that a League of Nations was formed to prevent the outbreak of further wars. Yet already Japan and China are fighting.

Though even now a far from admirable paragraph, it has at least a proper sequence of thought.

Paragraph-building Devices. (1) *Use of Connective Words.* To secure continuity, sentences may be linked by connecting words and phrases such as *however, moreover, nevertheless, yet, in addition, finally,* etc. Such expressions, when correctly used, provide links between the ideas of sentences which would otherwise be separated by an awkward gap. Yet the too frequent use of connectives may cause nearly as much awkwardness as too little. Moreover, they cannot be employed indiscriminately; each has a definite use. *However, nevertheless* and *yet* always have an adversative effect; they denote a contrast:

> He acknowledged, at a later period, that his success on this occasion was to be attributed, not at all to his own generalship, but solely to the valour and steadiness of his troops. He completely effaced, *however*, by his personal courage and energy, the stain which Mollwitz had left on his reputation.

Moreover and *in addition* are cumulative connectives; they introduce a statement additional to the preceding:

> When Mr. Stimson underlined the fact that he only recommended consultation as a means of " mobilising international opinion," the practical value of his contribution to Security was felt to be so much diminished that little was left. *Moreover*, even if the President made a personal unilateral declaration of what he himself would be prepared to do, he cannot bind his successors, nor can he guarantee its acceptance by Congress.

2. *Use of Sentence summing up the Foregoing Paragraph.* To end a paragraph with a sentence summing up its contents will often serve to emphasise important facts:

> Millions are killed in battle, and even non-combatants are not safe. Buildings are destroyed by air raids, civilians are suffocated by poison gas. Food supplies are cut off and countries are starved into submission. Starvation breeds disease, and dreadful pestilences carry off thousands of people. The effects of the destruction and economic chaos caused by warfare remain for years after the conclusion of hostilities. Such are some of the horrors of war.

First Paragraph. It is very important to begin an essay well, especially as a considerable part of the art of essay writing consists in gaining attention. This having been done, it is comparatively easy to maintain the interest. The function of the first paragraph is to create a favourable impression on the reader, to arouse his interest in the subject, and to show him that the ensuing essay is worth reading. A poor or commonplace opening will destroy any desire to read the essay, and prejudice him against it beforehand.

It is unwise to plunge straight into the treatment of the subject, since this will make the beginning unpleasantly abrupt. The first paragraph should be a neat, concise introduction to the subject. Note the word *concise*; if too much time is lost in coming to the point, the patience of the reader will be strained.

Do not begin by referring to the title in such a way as "*This* is a question on which there is much diversity of opinion," or "*This* may be defined as . . ." The title is not an integral part of the essay, and the latter must be begun as if the title did not exist.

Broadly speaking, we can divide introductory paragraphs into two classes :

1. *Indirect.* By this method something so striking or original is introduced that attention is seized at once, and there is an urge to read on in order to find out whither this unusual beginning will lead. This may be done by :

(a) *Quotation.* For this beginning to be successful, the quotation must be original. A hackneyed quotation is merely irritating. To begin an essay on *Beauty* by quoting :

"A thing of beauty is a joy for ever . . ." is merely to expose the limitations of the writer's reading.

(*b*) An anecdote illustrating some aspect of the subject to be considered. To succeed, this must be striking and concisely narrated.

(*c*) Some striking remark, often giving an unexpected twist to some popular saying; for example, the following opening sentence to an essay on Practical Jokes : " All the world loves a lover, but how much more does it love a joker ! "

(*d*) A paragraph apparently quite unconnected with the subject. E. V. Lucas begins his essay *Of Bareheadedness* thus :

> The motto on the play-bill of a recent comedy stated that kings and queens have five fingers on each hand, take their meals regularly, and are, in short, the same as other people. But it is not true. No amount of such assurance will make kings the same as other people, because they are not. And the reason that they are not the same is that they are different. I have just seen some of the difference.

This type of paragraph depends on a suspense effect. The reader is urged to read on in order to find out how this apparently irrelevant paragraph is connected with the subject. However, it needs considerable skill, and the beginner is not advised to attempt it; he should aim at coming to the point as soon as possible.

2. *Direct*. The methods we have outlined require a certain amount of originality and literary skill. They either succeed completely or fail. A less effective, but more generally efficient method for the beginner is to commence the essay with a clear, terse definition of the subject and scope of the essay. This requires no special ability, except that it should be done as interestingly as possible. The fault with this method is that it so easily

becomes dry and pompous. It creates a bad impression on the reader to begin in such style as : " I propose to consider the subject of . . ." or " In the following pages it is my purpose to treat of . . ." The beginning of Stevenson's essay on *Walking Tours* is a good example of the method; interesting in itself, and giving a clear idea of the subject :

It must not be imagined that a walking tour, as some would have it, is merely a better or worse way of seeing the country. There are many ways of seeing landscape quite as good ; and none more vivid, in spite of canting dilettantes, than from a railway train. But landscape on a walking tour is quite accessory. He who is indeed of the brotherhood does not voyage in quest of the picturesque, but of certain jolly humours —of the hope and spirit with which the march begins at morning, and of the peace and spiritual repletion of the evening's rest.

Concluding Paragraph. An essay must be brought to a conclusion; it must not just leave off, or break off apparently in the middle of the subject. It is the function of the concluding paragraph to give the essay completeness, to make it a finished whole, so that when the reader comes to the end, he feels that the essay really has ended. It smooths down the jagged ends of the argument or thought, makes clear the writer's conclusions, and brings the reader gently to earth after the flight through the essay.

There are several effective methods of ending an essay :

1. *A summary* of the writer's conclusions on the subject. This is the most widely useful, as the only quality necessary is the ability to think clearly, and yet it provides a very neat coping-stone for the structure of

the essay. A good example of this is Macaulay's summary of the life of Addison :

Such a mark of natural respect was due to the un-sullied statesman, to the accomplished scholar, to the master of pure English eloquence, to the consummate painter of life and manners. It was due, above all, to the great satirist, who alone knew how to use ridicule without abusing it, who, without inflicting a wound, effected a great social reform, and who reconciled wit and virtue, after a long and disastrous separation, during which wit had been led astray by profligacy and virtue by fanaticism.

2. *Eloquent climax*. This requires a considerable gift for writing, and will probably be beyond the powers of the average person. The conclusion to Stevenson's essay on *El Dorado* is a good example :

O toiling hands of mortals ! O unwearied feet travelling ye know not whither ! Soon, soon, it seems to you, you must come forth on some conspicuous hilltop, and but a little way further, against the setting sun, descry the spires of El Dorado. Little do ye know your own blessedness ; for to travel hopefully is a better thing than to arrive, and the true success is to labour.

3. *An epigram* expressing in a terse and striking manner the conclusion reached. This may be combined with other methods, as in the last sentence of the foregoing example.

4. *A question* is sometimes an effective close. If it is to provide a neat ending it must be very judiciously chosen ; in unpractised hands it may become clumsy. As a rule, the question implies a summary of the essay, as

in the conclusion of Aldous Huxley's essay *On Re-reading* " *Candide* " :

Il faut cultiver notre jardin. Yes, but suppose one begins to wonder why ?

QUESTIONS

1. Divide the following passages into suitable paragraphs :

(*a*) There are numbers in this city who live by writing new books; and yet there are thousands of volumes in every large library unread and forgotten. This, upon my arrival, was one of those contradictions which I was unable to account for. " Is it possible," said I, " that there should be any demand for new books, before those already published are read ? Can there be so many employed in producing a commodity with which the market is already overstocked, and with goods also better than any of modern manufacture ? " What at first appeared an inconsistency is a proof at once of this people's wisdom and refinement. Even allowing the works of their ancestors better written than theirs, yet those of the moderns acquire a real value, by being marked with the impression of the times. Antiquity has been in the possession of others, the present is our own; let us first, therefore, learn to know what belongs to ourselves, and then, if we have leisure, cast our reflections back to the reign of Shonou, who governed twenty thousand years before the creation of the moon. The volumes of antiquity, like medals, may very well serve to amuse the curious, but the works of the moderns, like the current coin of a kingdom, are much better for immediate use : the former are often prized above their intrinsic value, and kept with care; the latter seldom pass for more than they are worth, and are often subject to the merciless hands of sweating critics, and clipping compilers; the works of antiquity were ever praised, those of the moderns read; the treasures of our ancestors have our esteem, and we boast the passion; those of contemporary genius engage our heart, although we blush to own it. The visits we pay the former resemble those we pay the great; the ceremony is troublesome, and yet such as we would not choose to forego; our acquaintance with modern books is like sitting with a friend; our pride is not flattered in the interview, but it gives more internal satisfaction.

(b) In the early part of 1643, the shires lying in the neighbourhood of London, which were devoted to the cause of the Parliament were incessantly annoyed by Rupert and his cavalry. Essex had extended his lines so far that almost every point was vulnerable. The young prince, who, though not a great general, was an active and enterprising partisan, frequently surprised posts, burned villages, swept away cattle, and was again at Oxford before a force sufficient to encounter him could be assembled. The languid proceedings of Essex were loudly condemned by the troops. All the ardent and daring spirits in the parliamentary army were eager to have Hampden at their head. Had his life been prolonged, there is every reason to believe that the supreme command would have been entrusted to him. But it was decreed that, at this juncture, England should lose the only man who united perfect disinterestedness to eminent talents, the only man who, being capable of gaining the victory for her, was incapable of abusing that victory when gained. In the evening of the seventeenth of June, Rupert darted out of Oxford with his cavalry on a predatory expedition. At three in the morning of the following day, he attacked and dispersed a few parliamentary soldiers who lay at Postcombe. He then flew to Chinnor, burned the village, killed or took all the troops who were quartered there, and prepared to hurry back with his booty and prisoners to Oxford.

2. Criticise the following paragraph from the point of view of unity and order :

The most usual way among young men who have no resolution of their own, is first to ask one friend's advice and then follow it for a time; then to ask the advice of another and turn to that; so of a third, still unsteady, always changing. However, be assured that every change of this nature is for the worse. As it has been observed that none are better qualified to give others advice than those who have taken least of it themselves; so in this respect I find myself perfectly authorised to offer mine. In learning the useful part of every profession, very moderate abilities will suffice; even if the mind be a little balanced with stupidity, it may in this case be useful. People may tell you of your being unfit for some peculiar occupation in life; but heed them not; whatever employment you follow with perseverance and assiduity will be found fit for you; it will be your support in youth, and comfort in age. Great abilities have always been less serviceable to the possessors than moderate ones. To know one profession only is enough for one man to know; and this (whatever the professors may tell you to the contrary) is soon learned. Life has been compared to a race, but the allusion still improves by observing that the most swift are ever the least manageable. Be contented, therefore, with one good employment, for if you understand two at a time, people will give you business in neither.

CHAPTER V

STYLE

A WRITER'S style is his method of self-expression. All good writers have certain peculiarities of writing which give their works style, beauty and individuality. By the conscious and careful use of such features a writer attains the effects he desires.

Such command of language will be far beyond the capabilities of the average examination student. We shall not, therefore, concern ourselves with the literary beauties of style or the various types used by the great masters of prose. We shall content ourselves with indicating such simple rules and devices as will correct actual faults of style, and help to give a certain distinction to an essay and lift its style above the merely commonplace. One of the chief problems of the essay writer is to avoid boring the reader, and the use of simple stylistic devices will help him to avoid monotony and make his prose lively and interesting.

Simplicity. Beginners are apt to imagine that if they use as many long words and high-sounding phrases as possible, they are achieving a dignified and impressive style. They are quite wrong. Some of the finest prose, such as that of Bunyan and the Bible, is founded on the simplest language. Unless there is some definite reason to the contrary, always use the plainest language possible. Such language is nearly always more vigorous and hence more effective than elaborate, pompous phraseology. If great prose writers broke this rule, they knew the effect at which they were aiming, and the ordinary person will be well advised not to try to emulate them.

The most vigorous part of our vocabulary consists of those homely old English words which we use every day. The average style loses rather than gains from the substitution of long words borrowed from the Latin. The result is the style known as Johnsonese. Dr. Johnson was fond of long, sonorous Latin words, and wherever possible he used them instead of the more common English equivalents. The result was a pompous, inflated style, now generally condemned.

Avoid the unnecessary use of long words. Do not, for instance, unless for some definite reason, use *peregrination* for *ramble*, *epistle* for *letter*, *comprehend* for *understand*, *conflagration* for *fire*, etc., etc. Often long words are used for humorous purposes. Such attempts at humour nearly always fail. They are cheap and hackneyed, and should be avoided. They indicate the immature mind.

The substitution of clichés—popular phrases that have become stale and commonplace—for ordinary terms, is not recommended. A certain laziness and lack of originality in the choice of words are shown by the use of such expressions as *last but not least, to wend one's way, the Empire on which the sun never sets, mine host, our feathered friends*.

Hackneyed allusions are also an offence against simplicity. Instead of *Phoebus, King Neptune, the Emerald Isle*, it would be better to say plainly *the sun, the sea, Ireland*.

It must be stressed that although simplicity of diction is desirable, long words are not to be shunned altogether. Where an uncommon word will express the meaning more precisely than a common one; where it will express the sense of several words, even where it is preferable from the point of view of euphony, it should by all means be used. Simplicity does not mean that your prose should be a succession of monosyllables. Such a style would be intolerably monotonous and childish.

Conciseness. Brevity is an important point in composition. Always express your meaning in as few words as possible. The use of unnecessary words detracts from the vigour and effectiveness of the style, besides being a waste of time for both reader and writer. Brevity depends on two factors—the choice of words and the construction of sentences.

Choice of Words. Much of the art of choosing words consists in using those which best and most briefly express one's meaning. For this purpose a large vocabulary is a great advantage. With its aid it is often possible to use one word for an idea which less practised writers could only express by means of a clause. Be continually on the alert, and consider whether each idea could not be expressed more concisely and vigorously by alteration in the wording. For instance, the following sentence:

> Practical jokes are enjoyed both by those who play them and by those on whom they are played.

could be made much more neat and concise if the writer had paused for a moment over his choice of words, viz. :

> Practical jokes are enjoyed by both the perpetrators and their victims.

The models of conciseness are familiar proverbs and maxims quoted from famous writers. An essay must not be a series of epigrams; that would be absurd. It is, however, through their brevity and pithiness that these sayings have impressed themselves on the popular mind. Thus is the effectiveness of brevity illustrated.

Construction of Sentences. The following are a few devices which will help in the construction of concise, well-knit sentences :

1. Use of a noun in apposition in place of a relative or co-ordinate clause :

Dr. Johnson, *who was* the finest conversationalist of his day, first became famous as a lexicographer.

After walking for several hours we reached Chester, *which is* a fine old city on the Dee.

By the use of this device, the words in italics would be omitted as being understood.

2. Use of participles for clauses, either subordinate or co-ordinate :

Faced with considerable opposition, he was forced to abandon his plan—a short way of saying *because he was faced*, etc.

The Highlanders, having reached Derby, then decided to retreat—a simple way of saying : *The Highlanders had reached Derby and then decided to retreat.*

3. Use of compound words instead of clauses. Note the increased conciseness gained by the use of such compounds as : *air-minded, pleasure-loving, war-mongers.*

Offences against Brevity. 1. *The use of superfluous words.* This includes tautology—the use of superfluous words in the same grammatical relation—and pleonasm— the use of superfluous words not in the same grammatical relationship.

Examples of tautology are :

Professionals are often guilty of *unfair and foul* play. He was *utterly and completely* exhausted.

Examples of pleonasm are :
Ridiculously silly.
Entirely unique.

2. *Verbosity*—the use of a large number of words by which all vigour is lost; often the sense is obscured also.

We are within measurable distance of a catastrophe of the first magnitude.

3. *Superfluous Detail.* Details for a piece of description or narrative must be carefully selected. Such a composition is often spoilt by the inclusion of masses of unnecessary, commonplace detail. Detail must be relevant and significant; it must serve some purpose, whether to arouse the reader's interest or to enlighten him. Insignificant commonplaces do neither. For instance, in writing an account of a journey, a minute description of the commonplace preliminaries to a journey would be uninteresting, unimportant, unnecessary, and a waste of space and time.

4. *Repetition* of ideas already stated. This does not often occur in adjacent sentences, but frequently a writer repeats a statement he has made some way back, in apparent ignorance that he ever made it. This is a fault largely due to carelessness.

Euphony. A piece of prose should please the ear of the reader. The sentences must flow smoothly so that there are no jarring discords. A pleasing style is dependent on the rhythm, which, in turn, depends on the position of the pauses, and the actual sound of the words used. After some experience in writing, the ear will become practised, and will at once detect a discordant note or an awkward pause. Awkwardness, however, has certain definite causes and remedies, and careful attention to these will go far towards forming a pleasing style.

1. *Awkwardness in the choice of words.* This is due largely to a defective vocabulary, and frequently results in obscurity as well. Often when their precise shades of meaning are not fully understood, two words of the same family, or of similar but not identical meaning are confused :

> The unison of all the railways in the country will shortly take place. Say : *unification.*
>
> Nearly every man drives some sort of transport. Say : *vehicle.*

2. *Repetition of the same word.* Such repetition usually offends the ear of the reader.

> The day will come some day when aerial transport will be universal. *Time* should replace the second *day.*

So also may the repetition of similar sounds, though the actual words may be quite different. " Accompanied by a loud *crash,* he *dashed* into the room." But alliteration, that is, the beginning of a series of words with the same consonant, can sometimes be employed with telling effect as in a certain advertisement, *i.e.* " Builds Bonny Babies."

3. *The placing of words of the same part of speech next to each other ;* this creates awkwardness, especially in the case of adverbs and participles :

> He departed hastily, immediately.

But note :

> Hearing a noise and noticing a light in one of the rooms, I crept downstairs softly.

In this case the two participles are both in the same grammatical relationship to " I " and their proximity does not spoil the euphony of the sentence.

Note also the awkwardness often caused by the use of nouns as adjectives. The adjacent nouns destroy the euphony.

The coal industry representatives met yesterday. Say : *The representatives of the coal industry met yesterday.*

4. *Do not end a sentence with a preposition or other unemphatic word, if it can be avoided.* The beginning and end are the two most emphatic positions in the sentence, and an important word should be placed there.

That is the danger which I came to warn you against.

This is the bridge which the road to Scotland crosses over.

Against and *over* should precede the relative *which*.

Rhetorical Devices :

1. *Balanced Sentences :* Consider the following :

We censure the chiefs of the army for not yielding to popular opinion ; but we cannot censure Milton for wishing to change that opinion.

Note how each half of the sentence precisely balances the other ; for each important word in the first half there is a corresponding word in the second. Not only has such a balanced sentence symmetry and rhythm which greatly enhance its euphony, but also its construction makes it more effective. The balance gives it a force, which would be lacking in a less symmetrical sentence, and drives the point home. When a point needs to be effectively emphasised, the balanced sentence is a very useful device.

2. *Repetition :* When it is desired to impress a word or phrase very forcibly on the mind of the reader, it is effective to repeat the word.

But what shall we say *of* Addison's humour, *of* his sense of the ludicrous, *of* his power of awakening that sense in others, and *of* drawing mirth from incidents which occur every day ?

The repetition of the preposition *of* helps to emphasise the phrases which follow. Another example :

Britons never, never, never shall be slaves !

3. *Use of " it is " " it was,"* etc. It is often effective to begin a sentence in this way to emphasise the following words. It indicates clearly the part of the sentence on which the emphasis is to be placed. For instance : " It was to him that I turned in my distress," is much more emphatic, and the emphasis is much clearer than " I turned to him in my distress," or even, " To him I turned in my distress."

4. *Departure from Regular Order :* The last sentence quoted is an example of this.

5. *Recapitulation :* This sums up and emphasises the ideas which have gone before.

Disarmament, the Far Eastern situation, the unprecedented depression in trade—these are some of the problems confronting the world to-day.

6. *Use of " do,"* etc. A verb may often be effectively emphasised by the introduction of the auxiliary verb *do* :

They were four hungry schoolboys and eat they did.
He refused several times, but after all, he did consent.

The usage is illustrated by the story of the schoolboy, reading the Bible, who, coming to the expression "And they did eat——," immediately presumed that the use of *did* was emphatic as in present-day standard English, and pronounced the word with great stress.

7. *Use of Correlatives :* These include *either—or ; not only —but also ; although—yet.*

He is not only learned but also wise.

Although he was a man much buffeted by misfortune, yet he maintained a cheerful attitude towards life.

Either you will comply with my request, or I shall take steps to enforce it.

These sentences are much more vigorous and emphatic than :

He is learned and wise.

He was a man much buffeted by misfortune but he maintained a cheerful attitude towards life.

You will comply with my request, or I shall take steps to enforce it.

FIGURES OF SPEECH

Figurative language, judiciously used, adds greatly to the effectiveness of a style. A figure of speech may be defined as a departure from a straightforward statement, usually effected by the use of words in other than their literal sense. The following are the chief types of figure :

1. **Simile :** states that one thing *resembles* another. To compare one object with another gives the reader a much more vivid idea of what the author is trying to convey to his readers. To be effective, a simile must be striking and original :

He was like a living caricature.

Her hair fell over her shoulders like sunlit water dripping over the rocks.

Trite similes are best avoided. Such similes as *We ran like the wind ; he has a face like a monkey's,* are so familiar that they cease to be vivid, because they do not contain the element of surprise essential to an effective figure of speech.

Similes must be apt. Inappropriate similes, instead of illuminating the writer's meaning, often convey the wrong impression. Take, for example, the following : *Civilisation, like a fog, has encircled the world.* The natural inference from this simile is that the writer disapproves of civilisation, but such is by no means the case. Note the inappropriateness of the following simile to convey the monotonous indoor nature of office work : *Office workers are like wild beasts in a cage.*

2. **Metaphor:** is more direct and forceful than simile. It implies similarity, but whereas simile merely states that one thing *resembles* another, metaphor deliberately says that one thing is the same as another :

> *Simile :* " His intelligence is *like* that of a tortoise."
> *Metaphor :* " His intelligence *is* that of a tortoise."

Metaphors like *He is a Hercules in strength* are merely more direct and concise ways of saying : *His strength is like that of Hercules.*

Extravagant and elaborate metaphors should be avoided in prose. Far-fetched metaphors make for an artificial style ; they are like the artificial conceits of the Elizabethan and Metaphysical Poets. Elaborate metaphors are difficult to sustain, and soon lose their effect.

The mixing of metaphors must be avoided. This error arises where two totally different metaphors are used in reference to the same idea. The effect is almost always ridiculous, viz. : *The worker is a cog in the machine of industry, and must sink or swim with it.*

3. **Antithesis :** relies for its effect not on resemblance,

but on contrast. A good antithesis is usually a balanced, epigrammatical sentence in which two statements or ideas are shown in striking contrast :

> Democracy is the election by the *incompetent many* for the appointment of the *unscrupulous few.—Bernard Shaw.*
>
> A bird in the hand is worth two in the bush.

4. **Paradox** : is a statement which startles the reader by its apparent self-contradiction, if taken literally. On second thoughts, however, it is seen that the paradox conveys a considerable amount of truth. It is a form of epigram :

> James I was the wisest fool in Christendom.
>
> His fate was a living death.

Antithesis and Paradox should be used sparingly. They, the latter especially, are difficult to master, and their proper handling can only come from practice.

5. **Epigram** : is a short, witty statement, a piece of " potted wisdom " :

> All that glitters is not gold.

Many proverbs are really epigrams that have passed into everyday speech.

6. **Metonymy** : consists in the use of something associated with a thing for the thing itself, such as the Bench for the office of Judge, the Throne for the office of King, the Cloth for the office of Clergy. Note that these terms are used for the offices in general, not for a particular judge, king or clergyman.

7. **Synecdoche** : resembles Metonymy, but whereas Metonymy uses the name of something associated with the thing for the thing itself, Synecdoche uses the name

of something that forms an actual part of the original idea, or object:

Fifty *head* of cattle.

Bismarck's policy was *blood* and *iron*.

He had not a *roof* for his head.

8. **Climax :** here the ideas are so arranged that they gradually increase in importance from the first to the last:

I came, I saw, I conquered.

9. **Anticlimax :** is the opposite to the last; a sudden descent from the important, often from the sublime to the trivial. When intentional, this is often effective for purposes of humour, but care should be taken to avoid its unintentional use, or the result will be a laugh in the wrong place. The following contains several examples of this figure:

Whether the nymph shall break Diana's bow,
Or some frail china jar receive a blow :
Or stain her honour, *or her new brocade :*
Forget her prayers, *or miss a masquerade :*
Or lose her heart *or necklace* at a ball !

10. **Personification :** is a figure by which human qualities are given to abstract or inanimate objects. This figure is more common in poetry than in prose, but there are some quite common examples:

The ship set out on *her* journey.

All the world was asleep.

11. **Apostrophe :** an object or abstraction is addressed as if it were a person:

Ethereal minstrel ! Pilgrim of the sky !

O wild West Wind, thou breath of Autumn's being.

This again is a device more natural in poetry than in prose.

12. **Hyperbole :** exaggeration :

> He has *tons* of money.
> The noise must have been heard in Australia.

The use of this figure is *not* recommended.

13. **Litotes :** an under-statement, often by making a positive statement in a negative form :

> He is no light weight.
> He is by no means lacking in ability.

14. **Irony :** states the opposite meaning to that intended :

> He *modestly* claimed to be the bravest man in the world.
> For Brutus is an honourable man, so are they all, all honourable men.

15. **Euphemism :** states unpleasant facts in such a way, usually by circumlocution, that they appear less unpleasant.

> One of Addison's slight shortcomings was a tendency towards convivial excess.
> The chemical laboratory was permeated by an aroma not exactly reminiscent of a flower garden.

As a rule, this device is best left alone. It leads to cheap attempts at humour by the use of long words and circumlocution.

16. **Onomatopœia :** the use of words whose sound imitates what is being described or which creates the required atmosphere :

> The murmurous haunt of flies on summer eves.
> Like a glow-worm golden,
> In a dell of dew.
> A rippling brook.

This is a device more suited to poetry than to prose.

Other Points Conducive to an Interesting Style :

1. Be precise in detail, especially in description. Do not be vague or leave the outlines blurred. Adjectives should be chosen which give a clear-cut description. The picture is thus rendered much more vivid; the reader can visualise it clearly, whereas a description lacking in detail remains flat and blank.

2. Picturesqueness and originality of phraseology greatly help to bring the style to life. The happy, unexpected epithet or image intrigues the reader. To achieve this, a judicious choice of words is necessary. Eschew all flat or obvious adjectives; as a rule their meaning has become so vague by use that they are incapable of making an impression on the reader's mind. Such adjectives as *nice, nasty,* are often almost meaningless :

We had a very nice holiday.

What a nasty man !

We often find *beautiful* and *lovely* used where there is no sense of beauty in the accepted sense of the term :

My new car has a beautiful engine.

I was given a lovely bicycle for my birthday.

The meaning is not that the machines are æsthetically satisfying, but that they are efficient or easily operated.

Stevenson is particularly careful in his selection of the *mot juste*, and as examples of the art of happy phraseology, his essays cannot be bettered.

3. Humour is the spice not only of life but also of essay writing in its higher forms. Nothing is so delightful to the reader as true humour, but, unfortunately, this is very difficult to achieve. The gift of being effectively humorous on paper is not granted to everyone. If you possess it, it will greatly add to the effect of your prose;

otherwise, do not attempt this style. As a general rule, beginners should not attempt humorous treatment; the result is generally unsuccessful. Cheap or feeble attempts at humour are very irritating.

Points to be Avoided :

1. Journalese and other conventionalised, inflated styles. Journalese includes such faults as pomposity, the unnecessary use of long words, and an abundance of clichés. In journalism, too, we always find " we " used for " I," for journalism is a completely impersonal form of writing. The writer is not supposed to express his own opinions, but those of the journal in which he is writing. The essay, on the other hand, is the most personal form of prose, and the pompous journalistic " we " is not usually in place.

2. In avoiding pomposity, do not go to the other extreme, and become excessively colloquial. Slang should be generally avoided. It is inadvisable to break into dialogue in an essay. Beginners especially seem to be very fond of using the second person, and of referring to " the reader." This implies direct contact, and hence extreme familiarity with the reader. It should therefore be reserved for occasions when it is necessary to produce this effect, and not used indiscriminately.

3. Rhetorical devices when used excessively give an artificial, inflated style. Their too frequent use tends to diminish their effect and they merely tire and irritate the reader. Macaulay's style is apt to err in this respect. Rhetorical questions and exclamations are particularly apt to be overdone. These questions are a device of the preacher or lecturer, of the man who seeks to convince his listener or reader. They are not generally suitable for an essay, and if introduced at all should be used

very sparingly. Exclamations belong predominately to the sphere of the spoken word.

4. Exaggerated epithets. The careless use of such words as *awfully*, *frightfully*, *tremendous*, *terrible*, *terrific*, in colloquial speech is often reflected in writing. Such words should only be used when the sense demands words of their intensity of meaning, not where this is far too strong for the context, as :

> Be frightfully careful.
> How terribly exciting.
> I am awfully sorry.
> The holiday was a tremendous success.

Such usages show lack of thought and care in the choice of words and, moreover, they are absurd.

Suitability of Style to Subject :

Above all, the style must be suited to the subject. In the same way as one does not address a strange peer as one does one's intimate friends, so the style of an essay on " Christianity " should differ from that of one on " Jokes." Humour is out of place in dealing with a serious subject, as is solemnity in connection with a humorous one. Some subjects call for a light, lively style, others for a more full and serious note ; some for a plain statement of facts, others for a more embroidered style. Note the differences in style of the following paragraphs :

1. It would not be proper, for some reasons, to trouble the reader with the particulars of our adventures in these seas ; let it suffice to inform him that in our passage thence to the East Indies we were driven by a violent storm to the north-west of Van Diemen's Land. By an observation we found ourselves in the latitude 30° 2' south. Twelve of our crew were dead

F

by immoderate labour and ill food; the rest were in a very weak condition. On the fifth of November, which was the beginning of summer in those parts, the weather being very hazy, the seamen spied a rock within half a cable's length of the ship, but the wind was so strong that we were driven directly upon it, and immediately split. Six of the crew, of whom I was one, having let down the boat into the sea, made a shift to get clear of the ship and the rock. We rowed by my computation about three leagues, till we were able to work no longer, being already spent with labour while we were in the ship. We therefore trusted ourselves to the mercy of the waves, and in about half an hour the boat was overturned by a sudden flurry from the north. What became of my companions in the boat, as well as those who escaped upon the rock or were left in the vessel, I cannot tell, but conclude that they were all lost. For my part, I swam as fortune directed me, and was pushed forward by wind and tide. I often let my legs drop, but could feel no bottom; but when I was almost gone, and able to struggle no longer, I found myself within my depth; and by this time the storm was much abated.—Swift, *Gulliver's Travels*.

Here we have the plain, straightforward narrative style. It has many admirable qualities, and although the ordinary being can hardly hope to write as Swift does, he will do well to follow him in many respects. The language used is entirely simple and unadorned; this is an excellent quality in a narrative style, which does not generally need embellishments. The expression is very concise and vigorous; on reading this short passage we are surprised at the amount of ground covered. The

detail is very precise; not a point is left vague—for
instance, the position and date are given very accurately,
thereby making the narrative realistic and interesting.

   2. Just now, when everyone is bound, under pain of
a decree in absence convicting them of lése-respectability to enter on some lucrative profession, and
labour therein with something not far short of enthusiasm, a cry from the opposite party, who are content
when they have enough, and like to look on and enjoy
in the meanwhile, savours a little of bravado and
gasconade. And yet this should not be. Idleness, so
called, which does not consist in doing nothing, but in
doing a great deal not recognised in the dogmatic
formularies of the ruling class, has as good a right to
state its position as industry itself. It is admitted
that the presence of people who refuse to enter in the
great handicap race for sixpenny pieces is at once an
insult and a disenchantment to those who do. A fine
fellow (as we see so many) takes his determination,
votes for sixpences and in the emphatic Americanism,
" goes for " them. And while such an one is ploughing
distressfully up the road, it is not hard to understand
his resentment, when he perceives cool persons in the
meadows by the wayside, lying with a handkerchief
over their ears and a glass at their elbow.—Stevenson,
An Apology for Idlers.

This is a more graceful and " artificial " style. The
underlying vein of humour shows the effective use of this
quality in an essay. The effect is largely created by the
skilful phraseology and the vivid, unexpected imagery,
such as " lése-respectability," " the great handicap race
for sixpenny pieces." Originality of phrase and thought

such as that shown here adds a great deal to the interest of an essay.

3. The following paragraph shows many features of the good argumentative style. Note the use of telling analogy, and the clear-headed logic with which it is worked out. The style is plain and straightforward, yet the points are forcefully driven home :

It is not true that in all voluntary associations between two people, one of them must be absolute master; still less that the law must determine which of them it shall be. The most frequent case of voluntary association, next to marriage, is partnership in business; and it is not found or thought necessary to enact that, in every partnership, one partner shall have entire control over the concern, and the other shall be bound to obey his orders. No one would enter into partnership on terms which would subject him to the responsibilities of a principal, with only the powers or privileges of a clerk or agent. If the law dealt with other contracts as it does with marriage, it would ordain that one partner should administer the common business as if it was his private concern; that the others should have only delegated powers; and that this one should be designated by some general presumption of law, for example, as being the eldest. The law never does this; nor does experience show it to be necessary that any theoretical inequality of power should exist between the partners, or that the partnership should have any other conditions than what they may themselves appoint by their articles of agreement. Yet it might seem that the exclusive power might be conceded with less danger to the rights and interests of the inferior, in the case of partnership than in that of marriage, since he is free to cancel the power by withdrawing from the connexion. The wife has no such power, and even if she had, it is almost always desirable that she should try all measures before resorting to it.—John Stuart Mill, *On the Subjection of Women.*

4. Now we come to a more eloquent, elaborate style:

But Wentworth,—who ever names him without thinking of those harsh, dark features, ennobled by their expression into more than the majesty of an antique Jupiter; of that brow, that eye, that cheek, that lip, wherein, as in a chronicle, are written the events of many stormy and disastrous years, high enterprises accomplished, frightful dangers braved, powers unsparingly exercised, suffering unshrinkingly borne; of that fixed look, so full of severity, of mournful anxiety, of deep thought, of dauntless resolution, which seems at once to forebode and to defy a terrible fate, as it lowers on us from the living canvas of Vandyke?—Macaulay, *Essay on Hampden.*

There is no simplicity here; the passage is an elaborately constructed piece of eloquence—a purple patch, in fact. It is cited here as an illustration of the free use of rhetorical devices. The whole period is a rhetorical question. The impressive rhythm rises gradually to the climax reached in the words " a terrible fate." Among the more obvious devices may be noted also the repetition of the words " that " and " of," and the carefully preserved balance of nouns and adjectives—" high enterprises accomplished, frightful dangers braved, powers unsparingly exercised, suffering unshrinkingly borne."

CHAPTER VI

TYPES OF ESSAY

Essays may be divided into a number of different classes, each of which has its own problems of treatment. Their degrees of difficulty vary, and the candidate when in doubt, in the hurry of an examination, should, where possible, choose one of the easier types. He should, too, consider carefully the type of essay required for a given subject, although it must be remembered that many subjects are capable of various modes of treatment.

Narrative. A plain straightforward narrative is quite easy to write, as it entails no special problems of arrangement or treatment. It almost arranges itself, since events will naturally be narrated in chronological order. Difficulty is sometimes experienced in deciding on the positions of the paragraph divisions, as there are no very marked changes from topic to topic in an essay of this type. The best plan is to give a separate paragraph to each main stage in the narrative. The choice of detail, too, needs care, for particularly in narratives of personal experiences there is a tendency to include, even at length, utterly commonplace events which could be taken for granted. Above all, keep to the same tense throughout; do not suddenly switch over from past to present or from present to past for no reason at all.

When asked to write on, say, a journey of some sort—a fairly common subject—narrative treatment is obviously called for. It is far better to narrate a particular journey

than to discuss journeys in general. Subjects such as
" Walking " and " Angling " could be treated quite well
in the form of a narrative of some particular expedition,
although here it would perhaps be better to try some
more discursive method. In dealing with a subject like
" A Favourite Book," a purely narrative essay, compris-
ing a mere resumé of the story, is not really enough;
the various features which impressed us should be
emphasised.

Although a narrative is easy to compose, it needs
some fairly striking events as its material, if it is to be
interesting, unless the writer has sufficient talent to give
interest to the ordinary.

Historical. The historical may be regarded as a special
branch of the technical essay. Many historical subjects
admit of narrative treatment. For an essay of this type
a stock of accurate information is essential. Make sure
that you are really writing about the subject; if asked
for a discussion of a certain topic do not give merely a
plain narrative of events. Many historical subjects have
a very wide scope, and it is a common failing to attempt
to cover too much ground. If you are required to write
on a huge subject such as the French Revolution, do not
attempt to cover the whole ground; a mere sketchy list
of events will be all that is possible in a short essay. It
is far better to concentrate on some limited aspect of
the subject.

Descriptive. A description of, for instance, a landscape
or a season of the year, is fairly easy to write. The
chief aim should be vividness and picturesqueness. For
this, precise and clearly described detail is necessary.
The objects described must be clearly visualised by the
writer; immediately the description becomes vague and
blurred it loses its effect.

Technical. A technical essay may be described as one which aims at giving the reader a certain amount of information. Provided that one possesses a full and accurate knowledge of the subject, technical essays are quite easy to write. The arrangement is usually fairly straightforward. In subjects such as " Modern Methods of Communication " or " The Uses of Electricity " a number of fairly obvious paragraph headings present themselves.

There is a danger of being over-technical; a mass of very technical detail is not of great interest to the average reader. Again, it must be remembered that the reader is probably comparatively ignorant of the subject. The information must therefore be presented in a form which is perfectly intelligible to the layman.

Reflective. One of the most difficult kinds of essay is that which calls for reflection upon and discussion of a theme, such as " Friendship," " Beauty," " Literature " or " War." Yet when this type of essay is well done, it is most interesting. Here, problems of material and arrangement are considerable, and such an essay should not be attempted unless you have some definite, orderly ideas on the subject. Too often such essays are obscure, rambling, and lacking in a definite progression of thought. Clarity, consistency, and continuity of thought must be carefully maintained if the essay is to make a definite point.

Often a provocative quotation is given as a subject of discussion. Before attempting such an essay, make sure that you understand exactly the point of the quotation, for if you have not a clear conception of what you are talking about, it is reasonably certain also that the reader will not. Many essays of this nature are ruined by the writer's failure to define clearly the question at issue.

Argumentative. Certain controversial topics, such as " Sweepstakes," " Sunday Cinemas," " Nationalisation of Industry " and so on, are best treated in the form of an argument. The facts on each side should be presented impartially, and considered critically. It is then possible to arrive at a logical opinion on the matter. Your own conclusion should always be clear; a completely impersonal survey of the arguments is insipid and inconclusive. Aim at striking a happy mean between this and a heavily biassed attitude. Above all, do not confine yourself to stating only the side of the case with which you agree.

The most generally effective arrangement is to outline first the arguments on one side, then those on the other; each can then be criticised, and a definite opinion given.

Comparison. When the subject involves a comparison, for instance between two men, two countries or two pastimes, see that you really do compare the subjects under consideration. To describe each subject in turn, with a short paragraph at the end pointing out similarities and differences, is not a proper comparison. Similarities and points of difference should be brought out vividly throughout the whole of the essay.

Humorous. A humorous essay, when it is well done, is very effective indeed. Nearly all the great essayists, especially Lamb, have used humour. But it needs to be very delicately handled; too many attempts at humour are clumsy and cheap. If you can be funny successfully on paper, you are sure of writing an interesting essay. Literary humour is largely a gift, and, if you lack it, you will be very unwise to attempt an essay of this type. It requires considerable originality; the well-worn and obvious are even less funny on paper than in conversation.

SPECIMEN ESSAYS

The following essays, the first historical, the second a burlesque description, are merely examples of essays of their particular types. They are by no means intended as models to be strictly followed.

1. THE CHIVALRIC IDEAL

The schoolboy generally considers Richard I as an infinitely superior monarch to his father. The strong government, the beneficent reforms, the far-sighted statesmanship of Henry II leave him cold. Far easier is it to summon up enthusiasm for the picture of Richard Cœur de Lion riding to the rescue of fair ladies in distress, charging at the head of the hosts of noble Christian knights to rescue the Holy Land from the clutches of the barbarous heathen, and finally returning in triumph to rescue England from the rule of his brother. For Richard has been invested with all the glamour of romance; he stands as the model of courage, of courtesy, of piety : in short, he is admired as the incarnation of Chivalry.

The origin of Chivalry appears to have been the outcome of a reaction against the brutality of the Dark Ages. Military in idea, it aimed at giving warfare an atmosphere of idealism and lofty purpose lacking in the ignoble feuds which so often constitute the history of the preceding centuries. Chivalry was to be embodied in the Christian knight; he was to unite the courage of the Teuton with the idealism of the Christian, the honour of the barbarian with the justice of the civilised. The rule of might was to give place to the rule of right. The noble and strong were to protect the humble and weak. The era of selfishness and inhumanity was to give place to the era of generosity and courtesy. The service of petty military leaders was to give place to the service of the Holy Catholic Church. In short, materialism was to give place to idealism, and barbaric disorder to Christian order.

But this noble ideal, so noble as to be almost synonymous with that of Christianity itself, was destined never to be realised. The men who undertook to perform these prodigies of valour, these miracles of self-denial, were not lacking. They were bound to their purpose by an elaborate ceremonial typical of the Middle Ages, outwardly so beautiful, so pious, so noble; inwardly so grotesque, so insincere, so shallow. Equipped with all the regalia of the age of feudalism, the Chivalric knight sallied forth into the world to protect the feeble, to fight for the right, and to attack the powers of darkness. If even a modest proportion of those who took the vows of the Chivalric knight had carried out their ideals, how different would have been our attitude to Chivalry! But the initiatory oath was no more adhered to than was the oath of loyalty by Roger Casement. A knight protected the weak by proclaiming the beauty of somebody who had smiled upon him; he fought for the right by defending his own claim against all rivals; he attacked the heathen by wasting the energies of Europe in futile skirmishes in Palestine.

The ideal of Chivalry was to check the rule of might in an age of militarism. The knight was supposed to succour the feeble and prevent injustice. But in actual fact the helpless who were to be succoured never extended their bounds beyond one class which formed a small minority of the community. The miserable serf groaning under the tyranny of an overbearing lord never gained the support of the gallant knight to redress his wrongs. The knight never troubled about lending his services to the widow or the beggar. To him Chivalry meant the protection of damsels of noble birth from dangers which were sometimes real, but usually imaginary. According to Chivalric practice, the high-born lady was the only member of the community helpless enough to stand in need of the protection which his vows constrained the knight to accord. Such a perversion of the purpose of the Chivalric ideal would have been tragic had it not been so ridiculous. The reason for it is easily found; as the idea of Chivalry was being formulated, so Europe was suddenly awakening to the fact of woman's presence in society. During the rough and tumble of the Dark Ages, women had naturally occupied a very lowly station in life. The awakening of man's mind caused a violent reaction against this state of affairs. From being a slave, woman became a deity. This radical change caused a frantic search for a goddess who could be worshipped with a fervour which the knight found it impossible to accord the conventional all-male Trinity. As Christianity had no female deity, a substitute had to be found, and choice settled on the Virgin Mary, who became invested with all sorts of remarkable qualities. Thus the cult of the Virgin epitomises the Chivalric ideal as it was in practice.

In this way, from being a creed of universal application, Chivalry degenerated into a code of honour, etiquette and amusement for one class of people. The Chivalric knight, fighting for right and justice, degenerated into the gallant lover jousting for the hand of some worthless girl. The vow of fidelity and truthfulness was construed into a selfish insistence on knightly " honour " such as alienates Hotspur from our affections. " Honour " was apparently the exclusive possession of the knight, but from the trouble it gave, it cannot have been a very valuable one; it was a thing of such colossal magnitude

and such delicate composition that a rival could not open
his mouth without doing it some injury. Fortified with
his widespread but embarrassingly vulnerable rampart of
honour, the knight gave himself up to the insipid, worthless and ridiculous occupations of courting whatever
noble lady he happened to meet, and defending her
against imaginary dangers. Any reference to his fair
one by a possible rival was an affront to his honour, and
the offence must be expiated in the pompous, and picturesque but futile struggle of the tournament, where
many lances were broken, much armour was dented, but
little real damage was done.

All this pomposity into which Chivalry degenerated,
has not the appearance of being a great formative force
in history. It gave the young men of the time occupations which, worthless and ridiculous as they were,
probably did little positive harm. It provided an out-
let for the medieval passion for pageantry and display
which, however ludicrous, is probably little more amusing
than such modern occupations as foxhunting and horse-
racing may appear in five hundred years' time. In short,
the propagation of the Chivalric ideal utterly failed to
effect any change in the lives of the great majority of
the people, except that it increased the gap between the
upper and lower classes. But it had one or two results
not without importance. The most significant of these
was the interaction between the Chivalric ideal and the
change in the position of women. It has been seen how
this interaction perverted and circumscribed the purpose
of Chivalry. But the degeneration of Chivalry into the
idea of courtly love was a considerable factor in the
change of the position of woman.

In the Dark Ages woman had been a slave; in the
Chivalric age she became a goddess. She was put on a

pedestal and revered as the incarnation of beauty, sanctity and gentility. But although thus regarded, women were not allowed to put their various perfections to practical advantage. Lest their dazzling whiteness should be soiled by contact with mundane employments, these spotless creatures were permitted only one occupation : to receive the insipid and shallow attentions of the knights errant. In the circumstances it is a wonder that the whole upper-class population of Europe did not die of ennui long before the age of thirty. It is declared that in this respect Chivalry gave to women a more honourable position than at any previous period in history. Such a statement takes into account only a superficial view of the question. The position of woman under Chivalry was only less degrading than it had been during the centuries which followed the break-up of the Roman Empire, for the institution of a special order of society to protect her presumed that she was such a mentally and physically helpless creature as to be incapable of surviving any contact with the world. Only the most bigoted anti-feminist would deny that such an attitude was an unsurpassed insult.

The Crusades gave birth to the Chivalric ideal, and attempted to carry it out by defending the Church and attacking the faithless. But although the Crusaders fought nominally for the defence of the Holy Places and the spreading of the Christian religion, their motives were, generally speaking, of a far more worldly character. The quarrel of the leaders and the lack of unity of purpose, witness to the fact that they aimed more at indulging their medieval love of fighting than extending the Catholic Church. Even in the military orders in which the crusading and Chivalric spirit found its noblest expression, the same taint is noticeable. Moreover, it does not seem to have occurred to the Crusaders that it would have been far more in accordance with the Christian spirit to convert the souls of the heathen than to destroy their bodies.

The Chivalric ideal, setting out with the noble idea of making the world a better place for the poor, the oppressed and the weak, ended in a system of organised pandering to the tastes of the upper classes. To accommodate the medieval taste for romance, Chivalry invested woman and love with an airy romanticism popularised by the songs of the troubadours. To accommodate the medieval taste for fighting and pageantry, Chivalry organised futile Crusades and ridiculous tournaments. Chivalry was in theory a noble and beautiful illusion; in practice it was a ludicrous and fantastic reality.

2. The Newmarket Races

Of all the places of amusement where gentlemen and ladies are entertained, I have not yet been to visit Newmarket. This, I am told, is a large field, where, upon certain occasions, three or four horses are brought together, then set a running, and that horse which runs swiftest wins the wager.

This is reckoned a very polite and fashionable amusement here, much more followed by the nobility, than partridge fighting at Java, or paper kites at Madagascar; several of the great here, I am told, understand as much of farriery as their grooms, and a horse with any share of merit can never want a patron among the nobility.

We have a description of this entertainment almost every day in some of the gazettes, as for instance : " On such a day the Give and Take Plate was run for between his Grace's Crab, his Lordship's Periwinkle, and 'Squire Smackem's Slamerkin. All rode their own horses. There was the greatest concourse of nobility that has been known for several seasons. The odds were in favour of Crab in the beginning, but Slamerkin, after the first heat, seemed to have the match hollow; however, it was soon seen that Periwinkle improved in the wind, which at last turned out accordingly; Crab was run to a standstill, Slamerkin was knocked up, and Periwinkle was brought in with universal applause." Thus you see Periwinkle received universal applause, and, no doubt, his Lordship came in for some share of that praise that was so liberally bestowed upon Periwinkle. Sun of China! how glorious must the senator appear in his cap and leather breeches, his whip crossed in his mouth, and thus coming to his goal amongst the shouts of grooms, jockeys, stable bred dukes and degraded generals!

From the description of this princely amusement now transcribed, and from the great veneration I have for the character of its principal promoters, I make no doubt but I shall look upon a horse race with becoming reverence, predisposed as I am by a similar amusement, of which I have lately been a spectator; for just now I happened to have an opportunity of being present at a cart race.

Whether this contention between three carts of different parishes were promoted by a subscription among the nobility, or whether the grand jury in council assembled had gloriously combined to encourage plaustral merit, I cannot take upon me to determine, but certain it is, the whole was conducted with the utmost regularity and decorum, and the company, which made a brilliant appearance, were universally of opinion that the sport was high, the running fine, and the riders influenced by no bribe.

It was run on the road from London to a village called

Brentford, between a turnip cart, a dust cart, and a dung cart; each of the owners condescending to mount and be his own driver. The odds at starting were *dust* against *dung*, five to four; but after half a mile going, the knowing ones found themselves all on the wrong side, and it was *turnip* against the field, brass to silver.

Soon, however, the contest became more doubtful. The road re-echoed with the shouts of the spectators; Dung against Turnip; Turnip against Dung was now the universal cry; neck and neck; one rode lighter, but the other had more judgment. I could not but particularly observe the ardour with which the fair sex espoused the cause of the different riders on this occasion; one was charmed with the unwashed beauties of Dung; another was captivated with the patibulary aspect of Turnip; while, in the meantime, unfortunate gloomy Dust, who came whipping behind, was cheered by the encouragements of some, and pity of all.

The contention now continued for some time, without a possibility of determining to whom victory designed the prize. The winning post appeared in view, and he who drove the turnip cart, assured himself of success; and successful he might have been, had his horse been as ambitious as he; but in approaching a turn from the road, which led homewards, the horse fairly stood still, and refused to move a foot farther. The dung cart had scarce time to enjoy this temporary triumph, when it was pitched headlong into a ditch by the wayside, and the rider left to wallow in congenial mud. Dust in the meantime soon came up, and not being far from the post, came in amidst the shouts and exclamations of all the spectators; and greatly caressed by all the quality of Brentford. Fortune was kind only to one, who ought to have been favourable to all; each had peculiar merit.

G

each laboured hard to earn the prize, and each richly deserved the cart he drove.

I do not know whether this description may not have anticipated that which I intended giving of Newmarket. I am told there is little else to be seen even there. There may be some minute differences in the dress of the spectators, but none at all in their understandings; the quality of Brentford are as remarkable for politeness and delicacy as the breeders of Newmarket. The quality of Brentford drive their own carts, and the honourable fraternity of Newmarket ride their own horses. In short, the matches in one place are as rational as those in the other; and it is more than probable that turnips, dust, and dung are all that can be found to furnish out description in either.

Forgive me my friend, but a person like me, bred up in a philosophic seclusion, is apt to regard, perhaps with too much asperity, those occurrences which sink man below his station in Nature, and diminish the intrinsic value of humanity.

OLIVER GOLDSMITH.

This essay is a stinging satire on horse-racing. Goldsmith has not attempted to curb his scorn even though it offended the wealthy and influential racegoers of his time.

SUBJECTS FOR ESSAYS

Narrative.
1. A holiday cruise.
2. The autobiography of a shilling.
3. The most enjoyable day in my life.
4. A visit to an exhibition.
5. A great voyage of discovery.
6. The life of a butterfly.
7. The construction of the Panama Canal.

Historical.

1. The growth of British sea power in the sixteenth century.
2. Edmund Burke.
3. The influence of geography on history.
4. Roman Britain.
5. The medieval village.
6. Europe after the Napoleonic and Great Wars.

Technical.

1. Wireless.
2. Industrial psychology.
3. The Co-operative Movement.
4. Transport methods of the future.
5. The rôle of science in modern warfare.
6. Great inventions of the nineteenth century.
7. Modernism in Art.

Descriptive.

1. The country in spring.
2. The streets of London.
3. The present, as seen from a hundred years hence.
4. Country churches.
5. Impressions of a foreign country.
6. My hometown.
7. A modern Utopia.

Argumentative.

1. The good and bad effects of international sport.
2. The nationalisation of industry.
3. Sweepstakes.
4. Tariffs *versus* Free Trade.
5. The advantages and disadvantages of mass pro-duction.
6. Is democracy the best form of government ?
7. Is Rugby or Association Football the finer game ?

Comparison.

1. The contributions of Greece and Rome to human progress.
2. Europe before and after the Great War.
3. The advantages of town and country life.
4. Classicism and romanticism in literature.
5. Road and railway as a means of transport.
6. The plays of Galsworthy and Shaw.

Reflective.

1. Patriotism.
2. Traditions.
3. " The twentieth century is the age of noise."
4. " The child is father of the man."
5. Friendship.
6. " The true success is to labour."
7. Pedants.

Humorous.

1. Hats.
2. An imaginary visit to Hollywood.
3. The pleasures of idling.
4. Fashions in dress.
5. The disadvantages of punctuality.
6. A defence of murder stories.
7. Cranks.

The subjects appearing under the heading "Humorous" are merely meant as suggestions of topics which could be treated in a humorous manner.   They would equally well form the subjects of serious compositions.

CHAPTER VII

COMMON GRAMMATICAL ERRORS

THIS chapter is not intended to provide detailed instruction in English Grammar, but is merely a discourse on the errors most commonly committed in composition, and how they may be avoided. By steering clear of the pitfalls dealt with in this chapter your composition will at least be free from serious grammatical errors.

Agreement : 1. *Pronoun.* A pronoun must agree with its antecedent in number and person. A singular noun must be followed by a singular pronoun, a plural noun by a plural pronoun. Collective nouns like *team, council, number, club*, etc., are singular.

The *team* failed to do *itself* justice yesterday.

Such pronouns as *one, each, everyone, neither*, are also singular; it is a common error to make them plural :

Everyone has *their* own opinion.
One can choose whichever *they* please.

It is incorrect to use *he, him* or *his*, etc., after *one*; *one* is an indefinite pronoun, and can be followed only by similar forms. For instance, in the sentence : " One cannot tell what will happen to himself," *oneself* should be substituted for *himself*. In " When considering this question, one should adhere closely to his own ideas, and not be influenced by others," *his* should be *one's*.

The rule governing the agreement of the relative, which

is the same as for other pronouns, is often overlooked in such sentences as :

> He is one of those people who thinks he owns the world.

Who refers to *people*, and the clause *thinks he owns* should be *think they own*.

2. *Verb.* A verb must be of the same number and person as the subject.

A double subject, that is one consisting of more than one noun or noun equivalent, joined by a co-ordinating conjunction, is plural :

> Tom and Dick have gone out.

A collective noun or pronoun usually takes a singular verb. Thus : " The council have taken no steps in the matter," should be " The council has taken. etc."

> Neither of these *is* good enough.
>
> Each of the occupants of the house *has* gone out.
>
> Everyone *was* present.

Where the noun denotes not so much a single unit as a group composed of several individuals, it may be followed by a plural verb :

> The committee *have* disagreed several times.

" None " (= no one) is strictly singular, but it is now so commonly used in the plural that it would be pedantic to call this an error. The following is an example of the modern tendency to make it plural :

> None of the explorers *have* been seen since.

Influence of Proximity : When the verb is separated from the subject it is often wrongly attracted into the number of the nearest noun :

> He, together with three companions, *have* just gone away on holiday.

He is the subject of the verb *has*, but the close proximity of the plural noun " companions " has attracted it into the plural. *Has* should be substituted for *have*.

Where the provisional subject *there* is used, and the noun for which *there* stands is plural and separated from the verb, the latter is often attracted into the singular by *there*, which is regarded as singular. Actually, *there* is of the same number as the noun for which it stands.

There is, according to many people, greater opportunities for young men in the colonies than at home.

There stands instead of *opportunities* and is, therefore, plural. Thus *is* should be *are*.

Grammatical Consistency : (1) *Tense*. Do not change the tense in an arbitrary manner. If you begin an essay in the present, do not change suddenly to the past, unless the time at which the events took place necessitates this. Change of tense is justified only when the events take place at a different time from those which have been dealt with. For example :

I am told that he left yesterday.

I am told occurs in the present, but his leaving took place previously, hence the change of tense.

2. *Sequence of Tenses in Complex Sentences.* When the main verb is past tense the verb in the subordinate clause must be past tense also.

It *was* arranged that the meeting *should* be held on the following day.

He *decided* that it *was* not worth the risk.

I *remembered* that I *had* met him before.

Where the subordinate clause expresses something whose truth is universal and not confined to any particular time, the present may be used :

He *showed* by his example that a rolling stone *gathers* no moss.

After a conjunction of purpose *may* must be used where the main verb is present or future tense, *might* where it is past tense.

I *ran* hard in order that I *might* arrive in time.
I *shall* run hard in order that I *may* arrive in time.

In conditional sentences, the verb in the subordinate clause may be in the past or present tense. The tense is governed by the tense of the main verb. If the main verb is past and the subordinate clause expresses the future, the future in the past tense (*should, would*) must be used—the ordinary future (*shall, will*) can only be used after a present tense :

He *had* been informed that he *would* be required the following day.

but

He *has* been informed that he *will* be required to-morrow.

Thus it is wrong to say :

I shall be pleased if you *would* call to-morrow (*will*).

"*Should . . . would*" and "*shall . . . will*" are always paired as indicated.

3. *Person.* There must be some reason for every change of person. If you are writing in the first person do not arbitrarily change to the second, or to the use of the impersonal *one*.

Unattached Participle : The participle is a combination of verb and adjective. As it is an adjective, it must qualify some noun or noun equivalent. Therefore, in using a participle see that it is neither without a noun to qualify, nor attached to the wrong noun—the result of such wrong attachment is usually absurd :

Coming to the top of the hill, a house was seen in the valley below.

The participle *coming* should obviously qualify the people who were climbing the hill—the meaning being : *when we came to the top of the hill*. But, as it stands, *coming* qualifies *house*, giving the absurd meaning that the house had ascended the hill.

A wrongly attached participle can always be remedied by the substitution of a subordinate clause for the participial phrase.

The participle entirely unattached to any noun is often found at the end of a letter, *e.g.*

Hoping that you are quite well, yours sincerely.

There is no noun that *hoping* can qualify; it should obviously qualify the writer; therefore *I am* should be inserted between *well* and *yours*.

The Gerund : The Gerund and Present Participle both have the same form, and are often confused in construction. The former is a verbal *noun*, the latter, a verbal *adjective*. Therefore the gerund must be preceded not by the accusative but by the genitive or by a possessive adjective. For example :

I objected to him coming late.

is wrong. This sentence as it stands implies that I objected to *him, coming late* being merely a participial phrase qualifying *him*, whereas the meaning is obviously that *I objected to his action in coming late*. Hence *coming* is a noun—a gerund—and should be qualified by the possessive adjective *his*. Similarly, in :

The audience was delighted by the artist rendering the song so well.

Artist should be genitive—*artist's*.

Particular attention is drawn to this error, not only because it is common, but also because at first glance it may not appear to be an error at all—if the rule is not at our finger-tips, there is nothing obviously wrong with the sentences quoted. To complicate matters further, the form with the accusative is sometimes the correct one. In such cases it must be remembered that the form in *-ing* is a participle, not a gerund :

> The world expects much from the conference sitting in London.

In this sentence, *conference* is properly the accusative, object of *from*, and qualified by the participle *sitting*. The correct construction depends on whether the noun or pronoun, or the form in *-ing*, is the true object of the preposition.

Split Infinitive. The two parts of an infinitive—the preposition *to* and the verb—are so closely connected that they form grammatically one word. Therefore, although it is a common practice, they should not be divided by an adverb.

> He proceeded to calmly give orders.
> He was able to easily succeed.

would be much better written : *to give orders calmly ; to succeed easily.*

But the split infinitive is justifiable when it gives greater emphasis, or when any other order would create ambiguity or destroy the euphony of the sentence. For instance :

> The leader found it impossible really to control his followers.

is rather awkward; it would be less clumsy to write : *to really control.*

Note that in the passive infinitive, e.g. *to be promoted, to be liked*, an adverb may be placed between *be* and *promoted, liked ;* the infinitive is only split if the adverb is placed between *to* and *be*.

Confusion of Parts of Speech. *Like* is a preposition, and cannot be used as a conjunction. We cannot say :

The farmer works hard, like his fathers did before him.

Like must be replaced by *as*, or we can omit the verb *did*, when *like* would be correctly used as a preposition governing *fathers*.

After can be used as a preposition or conjunction, but not as an adverb. The corresponding adverb is *afterwards*. Thus it is incorrect to say :

I am going out now, I will call on you *after*.

After should be *afterwards*.

Nouns should not, as a general rule, be used as *adjectives*. Instead of : *This is the electricity age*, it would be better to say : *This is the electrical age*, or *This is the age of electricity*.

Above is an adverb or preposition, and cannot be used as an adjective. It is incorrect to say :

From the *above* statement we conclude——

Say : *foregoing*.

Pairs of Conjunctions. Such pairs of conjunctions as the following are often placed in the wrong position in the sentence. The second conjunction must be followed by the same parts of speech as the first.

Both—and : The following are incorrect :

He showed himself both as a fool and a rogue. (*Both* should follow *as*.)

Britain was both allied to France and to Russia
(*Both* should follow *allied*.)

Not only—but also :

The writer not only shows himself to be a stylist,
but also a thinker. (*Not only* should follow *be*).

This success not only reflects credit on the leader, but
also on all his followers. (*Not only* should follow *credit*.)

Either—or ; *neither—nor :*

The result will either be complete success or complete
failure. (*Be* should precede *either*.)

I neither said this nor anything like it. (*Said* should
precede *neither*.)

Note that *or* follows *either* and *nor* follows *neither*.

Comparison of Adjectives and Adverbs : *Double comparisons* must be avoided. The following are examples
of incorrect usage :

This is the more larger house of the two.

I am a more faster runner than you.

More is unnecessary in both sentences.

Similarly with double superlatives :

This is the most simplest method I have met.

Comparison of Adverbs. Adverbs of one syllable form
their comparative and superlative, like adjectives, by the
addition of the suffixes—*er*—*est : fast, faster, fastest ;
hard, harder, hardest.* Those ending in *-ly*, however, add
more or *most : quickly, more quickly, most quickly ; easily,
more easily, most easily.*

To use forms like *quicker, quickest, easier, easiest,* as
adverbs is incorrect.

Incomplete Comparisons. Do not use the comparative
unless two things are actually being compared. A
sentence like : *He is a faster runner,* is pointless, unless

some other runner is compared with him. To complete the sense we need to add, e.g. *than his brother*.

Miscellaneous Errors : *Same.* Avoid strictly the use of *same* in the following construction :

This is a great defect in the machine, and the inventors are trying to remedy *same*.

Use *it* or any other suitable construction rather than *same*.

Who and which. *Who* is only used in reference to human beings; it is often wrongly used in connection with abstract and collective nouns. In such sentences as the following *which* should be used instead of *who :*

This is the team who has won the most matches this season.

America, who, after the war, enjoyed a period of prosperity, is now suffering from a severe slump.

There is, however, a growing tendency to use *who* for countries and animals.

Who and whom. *Who* is the nominative, *whom* the accusative form. But it is to be remembered that the case of the relative depends on its function in *the clause it introduces*.

Thus in the following example :—

He made enquiries as to *whom* was the culprit.

Whom should be *who*, as it is the subject of the following clause, even though it may appear at first sight to be the object of the preposition *to*.

Providing that is often wrongly used for *provided that :*

Providing that there is sufficient public support, the scheme should be a success. (Use *provided* here, and not *providing*.)

Hardly and *scarcely* are often wrongly used with the negative :

I hadn't hardly time to catch the train.

Use of the Wrong Prepositions. Certain words can be followed only by some particular preposition. The following are a few of those most frequently confused :

Different *from*, not *to* or *than*.

We compare a thing *with* something similar, *e.g.* one make of car with another; but *to* something dissimilar, *e.g.* " He compared the country to a rudderless ship."

Superior *to*, not *than*.

Preferable *to*, not *than*.

Concerned *in* some business, not *with* ; *at* or *about* some accident; *for* somebody's welfare.

Common Sense in the Use of Words.   Howlers are often committed through the lack of attention to the meaning of expressions used.   Note the absurdity of the following :

His remarks on the subject touched the height of mediocrity.

La Bohème is by far the most popular of Puccini's operas, with *Madam Butterfly* a close second.

Horses are now used less universally than formerly.

No man's character showed greater depths of superficiality.

Height and *mediocrity* ; *depth* and *superficiality* are contradictions in terms; the second sentence is an obvious contradiction ; *universal* is one of those absolute terms—*perfect* and *essential* are others—which do not admit of degrees of comparison ; a thing is either *universal* or it is not.

QUESTIONS

Criticise and correct if necessary the following sentences :

1. He is fortunate by having won the prize.
2. People often employ badly the use of money.
3. I should be obliged if you will help me.
4. The conduct of men depends upon what they do with their time.
5. Forgive me talking in this way.
6. The term essay is a word with many shades of meaning.
7. Her sister gave her a book and her father a watch.
8. No one envies you more than your friends.
9. The mania for speculation now scarcely knew no bounds.
10. Too great a variety of studies distract the mind.
11. There is little fear of it becoming less universal in the future.
12. I never remember to have seen so beautiful a face.
13. People ceased to wonder by degrees.
14. My opinion is different to yours.
15. He is one of those who cannot describe what he does not see.
16. I never heard of you arriving here.
17. The four first competitors received a prize.
18. It follows as a consequence that we must act quickly.
19. I would be the veriest demagogue if I suggested that I had found a panacea for the immediate remedy of all these social ills.
20. After the most straitest sect of our religion I lived a Pharisee.
21. It is better for you and I as it is.
22. Adversity both teaches man to think and to feel.
23. This is one of those things that is managed better abroad.
24. Money is the most universal incitement of human misery.
25. He soared into the popular favour on a wave of popular enthusiasm.
26. He opened the door, and calling loudly, five or six soldiers ran to his side.
27. We must give the rewards only to those whom we believe have really merited them.

28 There was only two or three people present.

29. Both these words may be regarded as synonymous, the one quite as much as the other.

30. A large number of applications were received.

31. All commodities can be bought cheaper than ever.

32. Going down the valley, the scenery changed noticeably.

33. One always looks forward to their summer holiday.

34. He found that he could run much more quicker than he thought he could.

35. Taking a general view it seems to me that he is right.

36. I hope you will not fail like your brother did.

37. We have just introduced a new brand of tea and send you a sample of same.

38. I don't know which is the tallest, you or I.

39. There is no more unique stamp than this.

40. I not only expected him to come himself but also to bring friends with him.

41. His orders are that I should leave the house to-morrow.

42. The crowd who had collected gazed in admiration.

43. In consideration of the above statement there can be only one conclusion.

44. The horse used to be the only transport method.

45. Providing what you say is correct, the plan should be successful.

46. He suddenly realised that being Sunday, there was no need to get up.

47. We were astonished at him speaking as he did.

48. If I might be permitted to interrupt, I have a suggestion to make.

49. Neither of them are coming after all.

50. There is no country who desires war at present.

51. Not only is he a liar but also a thief.

52. On entering the building, the first thing that struck us was the great noise.

53. Everyone who saw the show said that they enjoyed it very much.

54. You will either obey me or I will punish you.

55. Not only did he arrive exhausted and half starving, but also in great pain from an injured leg.

SECTION II

PRÉCIS WRITING

CHAPTER VIII

PRÉCIS WRITING

What is a Précis ? A précis is a brief narrative, setting forth the salient points of some written data. The original may be a literary passage, a business document, a series of letters or any other type of matter.

The objects of a précis are :

(a) In business matters, to place the reader in possession of all the relevant facts without the necessity of his reading through the whole of the original matter. The chiefs of big businesses are busy men and must economise wherever possible.

(b) In examination work, to test the ability of candidates to understand the precise meaning of a piece of English composition.

Précis writing is assuming more and more importance in many examinations. In fact it may be said that the examinee who can write a good essay and a good précis, and has a reasonably large vocabulary, need not fear the result of his examination so far as the English paper is concerned.

In some examinations, especially those held by the Civil Service Commissioners, the question often asks for a summary, not a précis. In such cases, however, it is best to treat the two terms as synonymous, and, in writing the summary, to adhere to the rules of précis writing to be discussed in the following pages

The ability to write a good précis is largely a matter of practice—in fact constant practice is essential in order to attain proficiency, and the earnest student will, in addition to working the exercises given in this book, take every opportunity of making précis of literary passages and of economic and financial articles. The latter can always be found in good newspapers such as *The Times*, *The Daily Telegraph*, and *The Morning Post*.

Rules for Précis Writing. A good précis has certain characteristics which can, fortunately, be reduced to rules, and if these are memorised and applied intelligently, the result is certain to be passably good.

These rules are tabulated below and should be committed to memory. Illustrations and explanations of them will be given later on :

1. The précis must be written in good English, with a smooth flowing style. It is this characteristic which distinguishes a précis from a telegram or a summary. Any attempt to condense by omitting " and's " and " the's " or using telegraphic language will be heavily penalised.

2. Direct speech must be changed into indirect or reported speech. This matter will be dealt with at length in Chapter IX.

3. The past tense must be used, unless the sense of the passage requires otherwise.

4. The sense of the original must be rigidly adhered to.

Use of Past Tense. Such a sentence as, *e.g.*, The chairman said : " Things are much more satisfactory," would appear as " The chairman said things were much more satisfactory." This is because the chairman meant that things were much more satisfactory at the time when he was speaking. The précis is written some time after his statement, and therefore requires the use of the past tense.

However, such a sentence as the following : " Helium is heavier than hydrogen," would appear as stated, since otherwise it would seem as if it was intended to indicate that helium was in the past heavier than hydrogen, although not necessarily so at the present time.

Adherence to Sense of Original.   The writer of a précis has one object and one object only, *i.e.* to condense an original passage.   He may dispute statements of opinion, or even know that statements of fact are erroneous, but he must on no account alter them.   Even such an absurd statement as that the moon is made of green cheese must be rigidly adhered to.

Condensation.   There are two means by which condensation may be achieved :

1. By substituting words for phrases and phrases for sentences.

2. By omitting all that is irrelevant and unimportant.

Substitution of Words for Phrases.   This is largely a matter of practice plus the possession of a good vocabulary.   The following will show how this is done :

1. He is a *person who conducts ships in and out of harbour and along dangerous coasts.*   (He is a pilot.)

2. This window needs to be *furnished with glass.* (This window needs to be glazed.)

3. He was an adept in *the science of correct reasoning.* (He is an adept logician.)

4. *Inability to manage adroitly the feelings of persons dealt with,* is a cause of much dissatisfaction.   (Lack of tact is a cause of much dissatisfaction.)

In Nos. 1–3 a single word has been substituted for a

phrase. In No. 4 a little thought has enabled us to use three words instead of ten.

Substitution of Phrases for Sentences. This is merely an extension of the principle of substituting words for phrases. The following will show how this effects condensation :

> The motorist saw the oncoming lorry too late apparently to be able to avert disaster. However, he kept his head, realising that a head-on collision would probably be fatal, and with great presence of mind turned sharply into a ditch at the roadside. The result was that instead of a serious, and probably fatal, accident, the motorist escaped with a few minor cuts and bruises ; the only damage to his car was a badly bent mudguard.

Now let us try to condense the passage :

> Although apparently too late to avert a collision with the oncoming lorry, the motorist turned sharply into a roadside ditch, and, instead of being involved in a serious accident, escaped with slight injuries to both himself and his car.

In this version we have succeeded in reducing the length of the passage from seventy-six to thirty-nine words. If further pruning is necessary the passage can be still further reduced, viz. :

> Although apparently too late to avert a collision, the motorist turned sharply into a ditch, and escaped with slight injuries.

Note how the abbreviated passages compare with the original as regards what is omitted and what is retained.

Omission of the Irrelevant and Unimportant. This is a matter to which rules cannot be applied, since the question as to what is important and relevant and what is not must be settled by the writer. Rules could be laid down, but they would apply to certain types of matter, and in certain circumstances only. For instance, it may happen during negotiations for a contract that the original offer is rejected, re-made in different terms, and ultimately accepted with further amendments. Usually, it would be quite sufficient to set out the terms of the contract as ultimately concluded, unless, of course, the reader is likely to be interested in the preliminary negotiations.

A careful study of the examples given at the end of this chapter will serve to show how the unessential is discarded.

We know that each well-constructed paragraph has a main theme, and this may be taken as the most important part of the paragraph for the purpose of our précis. The question as to how much subsidiary matter is to be included must be settled by :

1. The permitted length of the précis (this is of paramount importance in examination work) and

2. The amount of detail which it is considered necessary to place before the reader.

Length of Précis. Usually in examination work, the required length of the précis is stated, *e.g.* " Make a précis not exceeding 150 words," " Your précis should not exceed one-third of the length of the original," or similar instructions.

Where the limit is stated, this must on no account be exceeded. On the other hand, there is no merit in condensing more stringently than is required to keep within the prescribed limits. Thus, if a précis of about 150 words is asked for, condensation into, say, eighty words would, instead of gaining special commendation, probably be penalised as not conforming to the requirements of the question.

Steps in Writing a Précis.   If a really good précis is to be produced it is necessary to proceed systematically, and the following rules are set out as being the most helpful in this connection :

1. Read through the whole passage in order to get an idea of what it is about.

2. Read through the passage again, and underline each important point that must be incorporated in the précis.

3. Make a rough draft of the passage, arranging the points underlined in appropriate order, and omitting all unnecessary matter.

4. Compare your draft with the original, and add anything of importance which has been omitted.

5. Check the approximate number of words in the draft to ensure that the number of words allowed is not exceeded.   If no maximum number is specified, the précis should be from a third to a quarter of the length of the original.

6. Read through the draft carefully to ensure that the matter flows smoothly, and that there are no grammatical mistakes.

7. Make a copy of the draft, and supply it with a suitable title.   The number of words should be given at the foot of the précis.

Simple Example.   Note that in some of the examples the important points are printed in italics.   They form the data which should be underlined for inclusion in the précis.

Write a précis of the following passage, reducing it to about one-third of its length :

St. Patrick, the Patron Saint of Ireland, the fifteen-hundredth anniversary of whose mission we celebrated last March, *is a mysterious and elusive figure.* It has even been *doubted if he ever existed* or, if he existed, how much of the *work attributed to him he performed.* A late ingenious dialectician has argued that he did exist and perform the work, but two centuries before the date assigned to him by traditional history. Nevertheless the perversities of modern critical scholarship have always failed against the plain witness of history, and we may be assured that we are *celebrating a real man* who lived at the time and *performed the work assigned to him,* and not a phantom of ecclesiastical propaganda or another man of the same name.

Tradition good and bad *has indeed had its way with him,* and he has shared the fate of many another hero of the Dark Ages and of the medieval time whose fame has come down to us strangely altered by the distorting medium of such traditions. For it is almost common form with the great men of those times that their very pre-eminence called into being different images of them in the minds of those who wrote about them *according to the different purposes which those writings were to serve. Charlemagne,* who lived on the dividing line between the Dark Ages and the dawning medieval centuries, is an excellent example of this principle. We know him more or less *as he was in history through the biography of Eginhard ; the Church legend of him we may read in the Monk of St. Gall* and the documents prepared for his canonization; and who does not know the *romantic figure of him celebrated in the epic songs of France ? These traditions cross and intermingle, but the different strands are plain to see.* So too *with St. Patrick. We have his own writings* carrying visibly upon their face the *witness of their authenticity.* And then, *at two centuries and more remove, the ecclesiastical tradition takes up the tale. The poets and romancers too must have their say,* and a *strange literature* gathers *round his fabled intercourse with the figures of pagan fancy and popular story.*

Précis

The Existence of St. Patrick

It has been doubted whether St. Patrick, Ireland's Patron Saint, whose fifteen-hundredth anniversary was celebrated in March, ever existed and if he did whether his works were authentic. The genuineness of both, however, is assured.

Tradition has distorted his true self as it has that of other early heroes, largely on account of the different purposes of various writers. Charlemagne as seen by Eginhard is not the Charlemagne of the Church or of the songs of France, although the links are clear. The same with St. Patrick. His own authentic writings are in existence; later, the ecclesiastics and poets and romancers took up the tale, with the result that a strange literature has gathered around his fabled association with mythology. (120 words.)

Example II (rather more advanced). Write a précis of the following :

Judge Jeffreys

The *depravity* of this man has passed into a proverb. Both *the great English parties have attacked his memory with emulous violence :* for the Whigs considered him as their most barbarous enemy ; and the Tories found it convenient to throw on him the blame of all the crimes which had sullied their triumph. A diligent and candid enquiry will show that *some frightful stories which have been told concerning him are false or exaggerated.* Yet the dispassionate historian will be able to make very little deduction from the vast mass of infamy with which the memory of the wicked judge has been loaded.

He was a man of *quick and vigorous parts,* but constitutionally *prone to insolence* and to the *angry passions.* When just emerging from boyhood he had risen into practice at the Old Bailey bar, a bar where advocates have always used a license of tongue unknown in Westminster Hall. Here, during many years, his chief business was to examine and cross-examine the most hardened miscreants of a great capital. Tenderness for others and respect for himself were feelings alike unknown to him. *He acquired a boundless command of the rhetoric in which the vulgar express hatred and contempt.* The profusion of maledictions and vituperative epithets which composed his vocabulary could hardly have been rivalled in the fish-market or the beargarden. His *countenance and his voice must always have been unamiable.* But these natural advantages—for such he seems to have thought them—he had improved to such a degree that there were few who, in his paroxysms of rage, could see or hear him without emotion. Impudence and ferocity sate upon his brow. The glare of his eyes had a fascination for the unhappy victim on whom they were fixed. Yet his brow and his eye were less terrible than the savage lines of his mouth. His yell of fury, as was said by one who had often heard it, sounded like the thunder of the judgment day. These qualifications he carried, while still a young man, from the bar to the bench. *He early became Common Serjeant,* and then *Recorder of London.* *As a judge at the City sessions he exhibited the same propensities* which afterwards, in a higher post, gained for him an unenviable immortality. Already might be remarked in him the most odious vice which is incident to human nature, a delight in misery merely as misery. There was a fiendish exultation in the way in which he pronounced sentence on offenders. Their weeping and imploring seemed to titillate him voluptuously; and he loved to scare them into fits by dilating with luxuriant amplification on all the details of what they were to suffer. . . .

His enemies could not deny that he *possessed some of the qualities of a great judge.* His legal knowledge, indeed, was merely such as he had picked up in practice of no very high kind. But he had one of those happily constituted *intellects* which, across labyrinths of sophistry, and through masses of immaterial facts, go *straight to the true point.* Of his intellect, however, he seldom had the full use. *Even in civil causes* his malevolent and *despotic temper perpetually disordered his judgment.* To enter his court was to enter the den of a wild beast, which none could tame, and which was as likely to be roused to rage by caresses as by attacks. *He frequently poured forth on plaintiffs and defendants, barristers and attorneys, witnesses and jurymen, torrents of frantic abuse, intermixed with oaths and curses.* His looks and tones had inspired terror when he was merely a young advocate struggling into practice. Now that he was at the head of the most formidable tribunal in the realm, there were few indeed who did not tremble before him. *Even when he was sober, his violence was sufficiently frightful.* But in general his reason was overclouded and his evil passions *stimulated by the fumes of intoxication.* His evenings were ordinarily given to revelry. But though wine at first seemed to soften his heart, the effect a few hours later was very different. He often came to the judgment seat, having kept the court waiting long, and yet having but half slept off his debauch, his cheeks on fire, his eyes staring like those of a maniac. When he was in this state, *his boon companions of the preceding night,* if they were wise, *kept out of his way* : for the recollection of the familiarity to which he had admitted them inflamed his malignity; and he was sure to take every opportunity of overwhelming them with execration and invective. Not the least odious of his many odious peculiarities was *the pleasure* which he took in *publicly browbeating and mortifying those* whom, in his fits of maudlin tenderness, *he had encouraged to presume on his favour.*

Précis

Judge Jeffreys

The depravity of Judge Jeffreys is proverbial, and his memory has been violently attacked by both Whigs and Tories. His faults have doubtless been exaggerated, but, in the main, the infamous character which he has been given is amply justified. He was quick and vigorous, although of an insolent and angry disposition. His vocabulary consisted largely of evil and abusive language, which he used freely and effectively without provocation. His expression and voice were awe-inspiring, and he took a delight in thoroughly scaring offenders with details of their fate. At an early age he became Common Serjeant and then Recorder of London, and as a judge of the City sessions showed his wicked inclinations. However, he did possess the one virtue of being able to get right to the point of a matter, but even this was usually over-clouded by his terrible temper. He was like a wild beast, and rained abuse and worse on all parties indiscriminately. When, as was usually the case, he was recovering from a debauch, his conduct was even worse than in his sober moments. In such a state he would turn with relish on his previous companions who had been the recipients of his drunken favours.

Notes on the Précis

The foregoing is rather less than one-quarter of the length of the original, which is quite reasonable for a précis of this nature. In such a passage as this a précis could be almost any length desired by the writer, since its essence is summed up in the single sentence " Judge Jeffreys was a terribly depraved man." The rest is merely a colourful embellishment and illustration of this fact. The passage can, therefore, logically be condensed into one paragraph.

QUESTIONS

When no special instructions are given, the précis should not usually exceed one-quarter of the length of the original. It should never be greater than one-third.

1. Rewrite the following passage, reducing it to about a third of its length :

I am just returned from Scotland, and after many journeys to that country I have been wondering what is the chief of the magnets that have attracted me ever since I first travelled there. A Scot bred and born might say that it was the heather; or a Highlander, perhaps, would answer that it was the hills, or both. But I find that it is not the heather or the mountains that I remember with most pleasure and look forward to most again, but the waters—the burns, the rivers, the lochs, and the sea.

Down through the granite and ling of a wide stretch of moor tumbles a little burn. Down from the moor, from tiny pool to pool, through blaeberry and bell-heather, by a green path of turf and rock, down to larger, deeper pools on the edge of the lodge garden. On the rim of the lawn stands a rowan tree, and beyond the rowan is a rickety wooden bridge, with the burn broadening under it over shingle, and the trout darting this way and that; and the burn runs beyond that bridge down to the floor of the glen, where it joins the river in a long dark pool of peat water, high with froth under the bank.

That is the first burn I saw in Scotland, and it goes with memories of other first sights of water among the hills. The Dee I saw first on a morning in March, with sunshine on new snow, and I remember that the river was as blue as a hedge-sparrow's egg under the white untrampled deserts. But close to the bridge the water was gold-brown, with bubbles under the falls hissing up from the deep, and the current curving by great boulders into clear levels between ridges of rock.

I saw the Tweed first on a day in October, and I think of it in three phases. One is linked with the vision of Eildon, "three crests against the saffron sky," and the broken arches of Melrose. That vision passes into another, as the evening darkens over the river, and on the broad dark stream yellow elm leaves float down to the cauld. And the third phase is in sunshine, the Tweed rippling dark blue under the sky of St. Luke's summer, or sienna-brown under the reflected riches of a great beech. To the Dee belongs the zest of spring in the Highlands, to the Tweed the mystery of the far-off years of the Border.

Of lochs I love best the lochans, the little lochs that lie in

pockets of the hills, so that you come on them without knowing that they are there, and see suddenly below you a saucer
of sunlight. And the other waters are those of the sea.
Not for me, first, the bright ripples of the Kyles of Bute,
nor even noon on the tides about the Hebrides, but the
sea as you may see it on the horizon, with heather bloom
in front of you and the Atlantic in a dip of distant hills.
That glimpse of the sea, too, is one of the magnets of Scotland, but for the strongest magnet of all I shall go back to
the burn.

2. Rewrite this passage in your own words, reducing it
to about 150–180 words.

Flood-water farming is practised to some extent in the
south-western part of the United States and adjacent parts
of Mexico. The Papago Indians, especially, are very skilful
in diverting storm waters at advantageous points by crude
ditches which lead the water upon subjacent tracts of level
land. At the beginning of the summer rains these Indians
make preparation for planting and cultivating their summer
crops by breaking the fallow ground left after harvesting
the preceding crops. In the loose soil thus prepared the
rainfall and the diverted storm waters are accumulated. In
it maize, beans, melons, pumpkins, and sorghum mature
rapidly under the influence of the warm summer season,
the moisture in the soil, and usually the continued rains
and floods of the summer.

In some places it is also possible to supplement rainfall
and flood waters with stored water impounded behind low
and inexpensive embankments thrown up at advantageous
points across marshy hollows leading from the mountains,
from which most of the water supply comes.

It is interesting to note the manner in which the Papago
stockmen adapt themselves to the arid conditions. About
July 1st, at the beginning of the summer rainy season, when
surface flood waters may be impounded in the valley bottom
lands, these people, with their cattle, horses, and agricultural
implements, move from the mountains to the valleys and
remain there, grazing their cattle on summer grasses and
planting quick-growing crops on soil soaken with flood

waters and occasionally moistened with rain. In the autumn, as the rains fail and the supplies of water impounded for domestic use disappear, the Indians go back to their villages in the adjacent foothills, where their cattle range through the winter on the summer growth of wild hay and are watered from their owners' wells. In this way, by spending half the year in the mountains and half in the valleys, these Indians live well in a region where white men, with methods unadapted to it, have repeatedly failed to establish themselves. The peculiar merit of the Indian method is that it shifts the cattle from mountains to valleys and from valleys to mountains each year, so that at no time are the pastures seriously overgrazed, as are the fixed grazing grounds commonly maintained by American stockmen.

Note.—In Nos. 3–6 the précis should be one-quarter to one-third the length of the original.

3. As to the wealth which the Colonies have drawn from the sea by their fisheries, you had all that matter fully opened at your bar. You surely thought those acquisitions of value, for they seemed even to excite your envy; and yet the spirit by which that enterprising employment has been exercised, ought rather, in my opinion, to have raised your esteem and admiration. And pray, Sir, what in the world is equal to it ? Pass by the other parts, and look at the manner in which the people of New England have of late carried on the Whale Fishery. Whilst we follow them among the tumbling mountains of ice, and behold them penetrating into the deepest frozen recesses of Hudson's Bay and Davis's Straits, whilst we are looking for them beneath the Arctic Circle, we hear that they have pierced into the opposite region of polar cold, that they are at the antipodes, and engaged under the frozen Serpent of the south. Falkland Island, which seemed too remote and romantic an object for the grasp of national ambition, is but a stage and resting-place in the progress of their victorious industry. Nor is the equinoctial heat more discouraging to them, than the accumulated winter of both the poles. We know that whilst some of them draw the

line and strike the harpoon on the coast of Africa, others run the longitude, and pursue their gigantic game along the coast of Brazil. No sea but what is vexed by their fisheries. No climate that is not witness to their toils. Neither the perseverance of Holland, nor the activity of France, nor the dexterous and firm sagacity of English enterprise, ever carried this most perilous mode of hardy industry to the extent to which it has been pushed by this recent people; a people who are still, as it were, but in the gristle, and not yet hardened into the bone of manhood. When I contemplate these things; when I know that the Colonies in general owe little or nothing to any care of ours, and that they are not squeezed into this happy form by the constraints of watchful and suspicious government, but that, through a wise and salutary neglect, a generous nature has been suffered to take her own way to perfection; when I reflect upon these effects, when I see how profitable they have been to us, I feel all the pride of power sink, and all presumption in the wisdom of human contrivances melt and die away within me. My rigour relents. I pardon something to the spirit of liberty.—EDMUND BURKE, *Conciliation with the Colonies.*

4. For although a poet, soaring in the high region of his fancies, with his garland and singing robes about him, might, without apology, speak more of himself than I mean to do; yet for me sitting here below in the cool element of prose, a mortal thing among many readers of no empyreal conceit, to venture and divulge unusual things of myself, I shall petition to the gentler sort, it may not be envy to me. I must say, therefore, that after I had from my first years, by the ceaseless diligence and care of my father, whom God recompense, been exercised to the tongues, and some sciences, as my age would suffer, by sundry masters and teachers, both at home and at the schools, it was found that whether aught was imposed me by them that had the overlooking, or betaken to of mine own choice in English, or other tongue, prosing or versing, but chiefly this latter, the style, by certain vital signs it had, was likely to live. But much latelier in the private academies of Italy, whither I was favoured to resort, perceiving that some trifles which I had in memory, composed

I

at under twenty or thereabout (for the manner is, that
every one must give some proof of his wit and reading
there), met with acceptance above what was looked for;
and other things, which I had shifted in scarcity of books
and conveniences to patch up amongst them, were received
with written encomiums, which the Italian is not forward
to bestow on men of this side the Alps; I began thus far to
assent both to them and divers of my friends here at home,
and not less to an inward prompting which now grew daily
upon me, that by labour and intent study (which I take to
be my portion in this life), joined with the strong pro-
pensity of nature, I might perhaps leave something so
written to aftertimes, as they should not willingly let it die.
These thoughts at once possessed me, and these other; that
if I were certain to write as men buy leases, for three lives
and downward, there ought no regard be sooner had, than
to God's glory, by the honour and instruction of my country.
For which cause, and not only for that I knew it would
be hard to arrive at the second rank among the Latins, I
applied myself to that resolution, which Aristo followed
against the persuasions of Bembo, to fix all the industry
and art I could unite to the adorning of my native tongue;
not to make verbal curiosities the end (that were a toil-
some vanity), but to be an interpreter and relater of the
best and sagest things among mine own citizens throughout
this island in the mother dialect. That what the greatest
and choicest wits of Athens, Rome, or modern Italy, and
those Hebrews of old did for their country, I, in my proportion, with this over and above, of being a Christian,
might do for mine : not caring to be once named abroad,
though perhaps I could attain to that, but content with
these British islands as my world; whose fortune hath
hitherto been, that if the Athenians, as some say, made
their small deeds great and renowned by their eloquent
writers, England hath had her noble achievements made
small by the unskilful handling of monks and mechanics.

Time serves not now, and perhaps I might seem too
profuse to give any certain account of what the mind at
home, in the spacious circuits of her musing, hath liberty
to propose to her self, though of highest hope and hardest
attempting; whether that epic form whereof the two poems

of Homer, and those other two of Virgil and Tasso, are a
diffuse, and the book of Job a brief model : or whether the
rules of Aristotle herein are strictly to be kept, or nature
to be followed, which in them that know art, and use judge-
ment, is no transgression, but an enriching of art : and
lastly, what king or knight, before the conquest, might be
chosen in whom to lay the pattern of a Christian hero.
And as Tasso gave to a prince of Italy his choice whether
he would command him to write of Godfrey's expedition
against the Infidels, or Belisarius against the Goths, or
Charlemain against the Lombards ; if to the instinct of
nature and the emboldening of art aught may be trusted,
and that there be nothing adverse in our climate, or the
fate of this age, it haply would be no rashness, from an
equal diligence and inclination, to present the like offer in
our own ancient stories. Or whether those dramatic con-
stitutions, wherein Sophocles and Euripides reign, shall be
found more doctrinal and exemplary to a nation. The
Scripture also affords us a divine pastoral drama in the
Song of Solomon, consisting of two persons, and a double
chorus, as Origen rightly judges. And the Apocalypse of
Saint John is the majestic image of a high and stately
tragedy, shutting up and intermingling her solemn scenes
and acts with a sevenfold chorus of hallelujahs and harping
symphonies : and this my opinion the grave authority of
Pareus, commenting that book, is sufficient to confirm.
Or if occasion shall lead, to imitate those magnific odes and
hymns, wherein Pindarus and Callimachus are in most
things worthy, some others in their frame judicious, in
their matter most an end faulty. But those frequent songs
throughout the law and prophets beyond all these, not in
their divine argument alone, but in the very critical art of
composition, may be easily made appear over all the kinds
of lyric poesy to be incomparable. These abilities, where-
soever they be found, are the inspired gift of God, rarely
bestowed, but yet to some (though most abuse) in every
nation : and are of power, beside the office of a pulpit, to
inbreed and cherish in a great people the seeds of virtue
and public civility, to allay the perturbations of the mind,
and set the affections in right tune ; to celebrate in glorious
and lofty hymns the throne and equipage of God's almighti-

ness, and what He works, and what He suffers to be wrought with high providence in His Church; to sing the victorious agonies of martyrs and saints, the deeds and triumphs of just and pious nations, doing valiantly through faith against the enemies of Christ; to deplore the general relapses of kingdoms and states from justice and God's true worship. Lastly, whatsoever in religion is holy and sublime, in virtue amiable or grave, whatsoever hath passion or admiration in all the changes of that which is called fortune from without, or the wily subtleties and refluxes of man's thoughts from within; all these things with a solid and treatable smoothness to point out and describe. Teaching over the whole book of sanctity and virtue, through all the instances of example, with such delight to those especially of soft and delicious temper, who will not so much as look upon Truth herself, unless they see her elegantly dressed; that whereas the paths of honesty and good life appear now rugged and difficult, though they be indeed easy and pleasant, they would then appear to all men both easy and pleasant, though they were rugged and difficult indeed. And what a benefit this would be to our youth and gentry, may be soon guessed by what we know of the corruption and bane which they suck in daily from the writings and interludes of libidinous and ignorant poetasters, who having scarce ever heard of that which is the main consistence of a true poem, the choice of such persons as they ought to introduce, and what is moral and decent to each one; do for the most part lay up vicious principles in sweet pills to be swallowed down, and make the taste of virtuous documents harsh and sour.—JOHN MILTON, *The Reason of Church Government.*

5. Write a précis of the following passage :

You will observe that, from Magna Charta to the Declaration of Right, it has been the uniform policy of our Constitution to claim and assert our liberties as an *entailed inheritance* derived to us from our forefathers, and to be transmitted to our posterity—as an estate specially belonging to the people of this kingdom, without any reference whatever to any other more general or prior right. By this means our Constitution preserves an unity in so great a diversity of its parts. We have an inheritable crown, an inheritable peerage, and a House of Commons and a people inheriting privileges, franchises, and liberties from a long line of ancestors.

This policy appears to me to be the result of profound reflection—or rather the happy effect of following Nature, which is wisdom without reflection, and above it. A spirit of innovation is generally the result of a selfish temper and confined views. People will not look forward to posterity who never look backward to their ancestors. Besides, the people of England well know that the idea of inheritance furnishes a sure principle of conservation, and a sure principle of transmission, without at all excluding a principle of improvement. It leaves acquisition free; but it secures what it acquires. Whatever advantages are obtained by a state proceeding on these maxims are locked fast as in a sort of family settlement, grasped as in a kind of mortmain for ever. By a constitutional policy working after the pattern of Nature we receive, we hold, we transmit our government and our privileges, in the same manner in which we enjoy and transmit our property and our lives. The institutions of policy, the goods of fortune, the gifts of Providence, are handed down to us, and from us, in the same course and order. Our political system is placed in a just correspondence and symmetry with the order of the world, and with the mode of existence decreed to a permanent body composed of transitory parts—wherein, by the disposition of a stupendous wisdom, moulding together the great mysterious incorporation of the human race, the whole, at one time, is never old or middle-aged or young, but, in a condition of unchangeable constancy, moves on through the varied tenor of perpetual decay, fall, renovation, and progression. Thus, by preserving the method of Nature in the conduct of the state, in what we improve we are never wholly new, in what we retain we are never wholly obsolete. By adhering in this manner and on those principles to our forefathers, we are guided, not by the superstition of antiquarians, but by the spirit of philosophic analogy. In this choice of inheritance we have given to our frame of polity the image of a relation in blood : bind-ing up the Constitution of our country with our dearest domestic ties; adopting our fundamental laws into the bosom of our family affections; keeping inseparable, and cherishing with the warmth of all their combined and mutually reflected charities, our state, our hearths, our sepulchres, and our altars.

Through the same plan of a conformity to Nature in our artificial institutions, and by calling in the aid of her unerring and powerful instincts to fortify the fallible and feeble contrivances of our reason, we have derived several other, and those no small benefits, from considering our liberties in the light of an inheritance. Always acting as if in the presence of canonized forefathers, the spirit of freedom, leading in itself to misrule and excess, is tempered with an awful gravity. This idea of a liberal descent inspires us with a sense of habitual native dignity, which prevents that upstart insolence almost inevitably adhering to and disgracing those who are the first acquirers of any distinction. By this means our liberty becomes a noble freedom. It carries an imposing and majestic aspect. It has a pedigree and illustrating ancestors. It has its bearings and its ensigns armorial. It has its gallery of portraits, its monumental inscriptions, its records, evidences and titles. We procure reverence to our civil institutions on the principle upon which Nature teaches us to revere individual men : on account of their age, and on account of those from whom they are descended. All your sophisters cannot produce anything better adapted to preserve a rational and manly freedom than the course that we have pursued, who have chosen our nature rather than our speculations, our breasts rather than our inventions, for the great conservatories and magazines of our rights and privileges.—EDMUND BURKE.

6. Write a précis of the following passage :

The place was worthy of such a trial. It was the great hall of William Rufus, the hall which had resounded with acclamations at the inauguration of thirty kings, the hall which had witnessed the just sentence of Bacon and the just absolution of Somers, the hall where the eloquence of Strafford had for a moment awed and melted a victorious party inflamed with just resentment, the hall where Charles had

confronted the High Court of Justice with the placid courage
which has half redeemed his fame. Neither military nor
civil pomp was wanting. The avenues were lined with
grenadiers. The streets were kept clear by cavalry. The
peers, robed in gold and ermine, were marshalled by the
heralds under Garter King-at-arms. The judges in their
vestments of state attended to give advice on points of law.
Near a hundred and seventy lords, three-fourths of the
Upper House as the Upper House then was, walked in
solemn order from their usual place of assembling to the
tribunal. The junior Baron present led the way, George
Eliott, Lord Heathfield, recently ennobled for his memor-
able defence of Gibraltar against the fleets and armies of
France and Spain. The long procession was closed by the
Duke of Norfolk, Earl Marshal of the realm, by the great
dignitaries, and by the brothers and sons of the King.
Last of all came the Prince of Wales, conspicuous by his
fine person and noble bearing. The grey old walls were
hung with scarlet. The long galleries were crowded by an
audience such as has rarely excited the fears or the emula-
tion of an orator. There were gathered together, from all
parts of a great, free, enlightened, and prosperous empire,
grace and female loveliness, wit and learning, the representatives of every science and of every art. There were
seated round the Queen the fair-haired young daughters of
the house of Brunswick. There the Ambassadors of great
Kings and Commonwealths gazed with admiration on a
spectacle which no other country in the world could present.
There Siddons, in the prime of her majestic beauty, looked
with emotion on a scene surpassing all the imitations of the
stage. There the historian of the Roman Empire thought
of the days when Cicero pleaded the cause of Sicily against
Verres, and when, before a senate which still retained some
show of freedom, Tacitus thundered against the oppressor
of Africa. There were seen, side by side, the greatest
painter and the greatest scholar of the age. The spectacle
had allured Reynolds from that easel which has preserved
to us the thoughtful foreheads of so many writers and
statesmen, and the sweet smiles of so many noble matrons.
It had induced Parr to suspend his labours in that dark
and profound mine from which he had extracted a vast

treasure of erudition, a treasure too often buried in the earth, too often paraded with injudicious and inelegant ostentation, but still precious, massive, and splendid There appeared the voluptuous charms of her to whom the heir of the throne had in secret plighted his faith. There too was she, the beautiful mother of a beautiful race, the Saint Cecilia whose delicate features, lighted up by love and music, art has rescued from the common decay. There were the members of that brilliant society which quoted, criticized, and exchanged repartees, under the rich peacock hangings of Mrs. Montague. And there the ladies whose lips, more persuasive than those of Fox himself, had carried the Westminster election against palace and treasury, shone round Georgiana, Duchess of Devonshire.

The Serjeants made proclamation. Hastings advanced to the bar, and bent his knee. The culprit was indeed not unworthy of that great presence. He had ruled an extensive and populous country, had made laws and treaties, had sent forth armies, had set up and pulled down princes. And in his high place he had so borne himself, that all had feared him, that most had loved him, and that hatred itself could deny him no title to glory, except virtue. He looked like a great man, and not like a bad man. A person small and emaciated, yet deriving dignity from a carriage which, while it indicated deference to the court, indicated also habitual self-possession and self-respect, a high and intellectual forehead, a brow pensive, but not gloomy, a mouth of inflexible decision, a face pale and worn, but serene, on which was written, as legibly as under the picture in the council-chamber at Calcutta, *Mens aequa in arduis*; such was the aspect with which the great Proconsul presented himself to his judges.

His counsel accompanied him, men all of whom were afterwards raised by their talents and learning to the highest posts in their profession, the bold and strong-minded Law, afterwards Chief Justice of the King's Bench; the more humane and eloquent Dallas, afterwards Chief Justice of the Common Pleas; and Plomer who, near twenty years later, successfully conducted in the same high court the defence of Lord Melville, and subsequently became Vice-Chancellor and Master of the Rolls

But neither the culprit nor his advocates attracted so much notice as the accusers. In the midst of the blaze of red drapery, a space had been fitted up with green benches and tables for the Commons. The managers, with Burke at their head, appeared in full dress. The collectors of gossip did not fail to remark that even Fox, generally so regardless of his appearance, had paid to the illustrious tribunal the compliment of wearing a bag and sword. Pitt had refused to be one of the conductors of the impeachment; and his commanding, copious, and sonorous eloquence was wanting to that great muster of various talents. Age and blindness had unfitted Lord North for the duties of a public prosecutor; and his friends were left without the help of his excellent sense, his tact and his urbanity. But in spite of the absence of these two distinguished members of the Lower House, the box in which the managers stood contained an array of speakers such as perhaps had not appeared together since the great age of Athenian eloquence. There were Fox and Sheridan, the English Demosthenes and the English Hyperides. There was Burke, ignorant, indeed, or negligent of the art of adapting his reasonings and his style to the capacity and taste of his hearers, but in amplitude of comprehension and richness of imagination superior to every orator, ancient or modern. There, with eyes reverentially fixed on Burke, appeared the finest gentleman of the age, his form developed by every manly exercise, his face beaming with intelligence and spirit, the ingenious, the chivalrous, the high-souled Windham. Nor, though surrounded by such men, did the youngest manager pass unnoticed. At an age when most of those who distinguish themselves in life are still contending for prizes and fellowships at college, he had won for himself a conspicuous place in Parliament. No advantage of fortune or connexion was wanting that could set off to the height his splendid talents and his unblemished honour. At twenty-three he had been thought worthy to be ranked with the veteran statesmen who appeared as the delegates of the British Commons, at the bar of the British nobility. All who stood at that bar, save him alone, are gone, culprit, advocates, accusers. To the generation which is now in the vigour of life, he is the sole representative of a great age which has passed away.

But those who, within the last ten years, have listened with delight, till the morning sun shone on the tapestrise of the House of Lords, to the lofty and animated eloquence of Charles, Earl Grey, are able to form some estimate of the powers of a race of men among whom he was not the foremost.—MACAULAY, *Essay on Warren Hastings.*

CHAPTER IX

PRÉCIS WRITING (*continued*)

HAVING studied the principles of simple précis writing we may now proceed to the next step, *i.e.* the conversion of direct into indirect speech. This matter has already been touched upon in Chapter VIII, and it remains to be seen how the conversion is effected.

Direct speech is that which is written in the first and second person, *e.g.* : " Well," said James, " and how are you getting on with your new job ? " " Fine," replied his friend, " and I am expecting a substantial rise in the near future."

The foregoing in indirect speech would appear as :

James asked his friend how he was getting on with his new job, and the latter replied that he was doing very well, and expected to receive a substantial rise in the near future.

Where we are asked to make a précis of a passage written in direct speech we have, besides effecting the necessary condensation, to change the matter into indirect speech. This, however, is not such an additional burden as it may seem, since, with a little practice, the transformation is effected automatically when writing out the rough draft.

There are a few rules which will be found to be of assistance in the rapid conversion into indirect speech :

1. When colloquial language is used in direct speech,

a more formal wording should be substituted. In the example the word *fine* is quite suitable in dialogue, but entirely out of place in reported speech.

2. The rules of précis writing as to third person and past tense must be followed. This applies whether a précis is to be written, or whether the exercise is a simple conversion from direct into indirect speech without any condensation whatever.

3. The passage must commence with an introductory phrase, such as *He asked; He wished; He stated; The speaker remarked*, etc., according to the context of the passage.

4. Terms of address such as *Ladies and Gentlemen; My dear friends; Brother workers; My Lords*, which are often found in direct speech, should be omitted entirely.

5. The wording of the original may be altered or re-arranged so far as is necessary to effect the change, but it must not be mutilated unnecessarily.

The following examples commence with the simplest kind of conversion, and proceed step by step to a fairly difficult précis of a passage written in direct speech. Needless to say, they should be studied with great care.

Example I.—Conversion of simple dialogue into indirect speech :

Customer : " Can I get a garden roller in this shop ? "
Assistant : " Yes, Sir, in our hardware department."
Customer : " And how do I get there ? "
Assistant : " It is on the third floor."
Customer : " Is there a lift, or must I take the stairs ? "
Assistant : " There is a lift. Through the door facing you and the first turning on the left."

Indirect speech.—A customer enquired whether the

shop in which he was sold garden rollers, and was told by the assistant that they did so in their hardware department on the third floor. He was informed that he could reach this by taking the lift situated in the first turning on the left through the door facing him.

Example II.—Somewhat more advanced:

" I have not been feeling at all easy in my mind until to-day," said Smith to his friend Brown. " My speculations have not been going well, but thanks to a kind friend, I feel I can look forward to the future with renewed hope." " That is splendid," replied Brown. " I am always glad to hear of a colleague who has been able to weather the storm. I have had setbacks myself, and can fully appreciate how you must have felt when things were blackest."

Indirect speech.—Smith told his colleague Brown that he had been feeling uneasy in mind until that day. His speculations had not been going at all well, but through the offices of a kind friend he was able to look forward to the future with renewed hope. Brown expressed his warm approbation of this good news, saying he was always glad to hear of a colleague who had weathered the storm. He had himself had setbacks, and could fully appreciate how Smith must have felt when things were blackest.

It will be seen that the first example is constructed in the same way as the dialogue of a play, whereas the second follows the construction of a story. The rules for conversion are exactly the same in each case.

Example III.—Précis of a passage written in direct speech. The salient points are printed in italics:

The next day opened a new scene at Longbourn. *Mr. Collins* made his declaration in form. Having resolved

to do it without loss of time, as his leave of absence extended
only to the following Saturday, and having no feelings of
diffidence to make it distressing to himself even at the
moment, he set about it in a very orderly manner, with all
the observances which he supposed a regular part of the
business. On finding Mrs. Bennet, Elizabeth, and one of
the younger girls together, *soon after breakfast*, he addressed
the mother in these words :

"May I hope, madam, for your interest with your *fair
daughter Elizabeth, when I solicit for the honour of a private
audience* with her in the course of this morning ? "

Before Elizabeth had time for anything but a blush of
surprise, Mrs. Bennet instantly answered :

"Oh dear !—Yes—certainly.—I am sure Lizzy will be
very happy—I am sure she can have no objection.—Come,
Kitty, I want you upstairs." And gathering her work
together, she was hastening away, when Elizabeth called
out :

"Dear ma'am, do not go.—I beg you will not go.—Mr.
Collins must excuse me.—*He can have nothing to say to me
that anybody need not hear.* I am going away myself."

"No, no, nonsense, Lizzy.—I desire you will stay where
you are."—And upon Elizabeth's seeming really, with
vexed and embarrassed looks, about to escape, she added,
"*Lizzy, I insist upon your staying and hearing Mr. Collins.*"

Elizabeth would not oppose such an injunction—and a
moment's consideration making her also sensible that it
would be wisest to get it over as soon and as quietly as
possible, she sat down again, and tried to conceal by in-
cessant employment the feelings which were divided between
distress and diversion. Mrs. Bennet and Kitty walked off,
and as soon as they were gone Mr. Collins began.

"Believe me, my dear Miss Elizabeth, that your modesty,
so far from doing you any disservice, rather adds to your
other perfections. You would have been less amiable in
my eyes had there *not* been this little unwillingness ; but
allow me to assure you that I have your respected mother's
permission for this address. You can hardly doubt the
purport of my discourse, however your natural delicacy
may lead you to dissemble ; my attentions have been too
marked to be mistaken. Almost as soon as I entered the

house *I singled you out as the companion of my future life.*
But before I am run away with by my feelings on this
subject, perhaps it would be advisable for me to state my
reasons for marrying—and moreover for coming into
Hertfordshire with the design of selecting a wife, as I
certainly did."

The idea of Mr. Collins, with all his solemn composure,
being run away with by his feelings, made Elizabeth so near
laughing that she could not use the short pause he allowed
in any attempt to stop him farther, and he continued :

" *My reasons for marrying are, first, that I think it a right
thing for every clergyman in easy circumstances* (*like myself*)
to set the example of matrimony in his parish. Secondly, that
*I am convinced it will add very greatly to my happiness ; and
thirdly*—which perhaps I ought to have mentioned earlier,
that it is the particular advice and *recommendation of the*
very noble lady whom I have the honour of calling *patroness.*
Twice has she condescended to give me her opinion (unasked
too !) on this subject ; and it was but the very Saturday
night before I left Hunsford—between our pools at quadrille,
while Mrs. Jenkinson was arranging Miss de Bourgh's foot-
stool, that she said, ' Mr. Collins, you must marry. A
clergyman like you must marry.—*Choose properly, choose
a gentlewoman for my sake ;* and for your *own,* let her be
an active, useful sort of person, not brought up high, but
able to make a small income go a good way. This is my
advice. Find such a woman as soon as you can, bring her
to Hunsford, and I will visit her.' Allow me, by the way,
to observe, my fair cousin, that I do not reckon the notice
and kindness of Lady Catherine de Bourgh as among the
least of the advantages in my power to offer. You will
find her manners beyond anything I can describe ; and your
wit and vivacity I think must be acceptable to her, especially
when tempered with the silence and respect which her rank
will inevitably excite. *Thus much for my general intention
in favour of matrimony* ; it remains to be told why my views
were directed to Longbourn instead of my own neighbourhood, where I assure you there are many amiable young
women. But the fact is, that being, as *I am, to inherit this
estate* after the death of your honoured father (who, however, may live many years longer), I could not satisfy myself

without resolving to *choose a wife from among his daughters, that the loss to them might be as little as possible,* when the melancholy event takes place—which, however, as I have already said, may not be for several years. This has been my motive, my fair cousin, and I flatter myself it will not sink me in your esteem. And now nothing remains for me but to assure you in the most animated language of *the violence of my affection.* To fortune I am perfectly indifferent, and shall make no demand of that nature on your father, since I am well aware that it could not be complied with; and that *one thousand pounds* in the *4 per cents.* which will not be yours till after your mother's decease, is all that you may ever be entitled to. On that head, therefore, I shall be uniformly silent; and you may assure yourself that no ungenerous reproach shall ever pass my lips when we are married."

It was absolutely necessary to *interrupt him* now.

"You are too hasty, sir," she cried. "You forget that I have made no answer. Let me do it without further loss of time. Accept my thanks for the compliment you are paying me. I am very sensible of the honour of your proposals, but *it is impossible for me to do otherwise than decline them.*"

"I am not now to learn," replied Mr. Collins, with a formal wave of the hand, "that *it is usual with young ladies to reject the addresses of the man whom they secretly mean to accept,* when he first applies for their favour; and that sometimes the refusal is *repeated a second or even a third time.* I am therefore by no means discouraged by what you have just said, and shall hope to lead you to the altar ere long."

"Upon my word, sir," cried Elizabeth, "your hope is rather an extraordinary one after my declaration. I do assure you that *I am not one of those young ladies* (if such young ladies there are) who are so daring as to risk their happiness on the chance of being asked a second time. I am perfectly serious in my refusal.—*You could not make* me *happy,* and I am convinced that *I am the last woman in the world who would make* you *so.*—Nay, were your friend Lady Catherine to know me, I am persuaded she would find me in every respect *ill qualified for the situation.*"

" Were it certain that Lady Catherine would think so,"
said Mr. Collins very gravely—" but I cannot imagine that
her ladyship would at all disapprove of you. And you
may be certain that when I have the honour of seeing her
again *I shall speak in the highest terms of your modesty,
economy, and other amiable qualifications.*"

" Indeed, Mr. Collins, all praise of me will be unnecessary.
You must give me leave to judge for myself, and pay me the
compliment of believing what I say. I wish you very happy
and very rich, and by refusing your hand, do all in my
power to prevent your being otherwise. In making me the
offer, *you must have satisfied the delicacy of your feelings
with regard to my family, and may take possession of Longbourn
estate whenever it falls, without any self-reproach.* This
matter may be considered, therefore, as finally settled."
And rising as she thus spoke, she would have quitted the
room, had not Mr. Collins thus addressed her :

" When I do myself the honour of *speaking to you next
on the subject I shall hope to receive a more favourable answer*
than you have now given me ; though I am far from accusing
you of cruelty at present, because I know it to be the
established custom of your sex to reject a man on the first
application, and perhaps you have even now said as much
to encourage my suit as would be consistent with the true
delicacy of the female character."

" Really, Mr. Collins," cried Elizabeth with some warmth,
" you puzzle me exceedingly. If what I have hitherto said
can appear to you in the form of encouragement, *I know
not how to express my refusal in such a way as may convince
you of its being one.*"

" You must give me leave to flatter myself, my dear
cousin, that your refusal of my addresses is merely words
of course. My reasons for believing it are briefly these :
*It does not appear to me that my hand is unworthy your
acceptance, or that the establishment I can offer would be
any other than highly desirable. My situation in life, my
connexions with the family of de Bourgh, and my relationship
to your own, are circumstances highly in my favour* ; and you
should take it into further consideration that in *spite of
your manifold attractions, it is by no means certain that
another offer of marriage may ever be made to you. Your*

K

portion is unhappily so small that it will in all likelihood undo the effects of your loveliness and amiable qualifications. As I must therefore conclude that you are not serious in your rejection of me, I shall choose to attribute it to your wish of increasing my love by suspense, according to the usual practice of elegant females."

" I do assure you, sir, that I have *no pretensions* whatever *to that kind of elegance which consists in tormenting a respectable man.* I would rather be paid the compliment of *being believed sincere.* I thank you again and again for the honour you have done me in your proposals, but to accept them is absolutely impossible. My feelings in every respect forbid it. Can I speak plainer ? Do not consider me now as an elegant female intending to plague you, but as a rational creature speaking the truth from her heart."

" You are uniformly charming ! " cried he, with an air of awkward gallantry; " and *I am persuaded that when sanctioned by the express authority of both your excellent parents, my proposals will not fail of being acceptable.*"

To such perseverance in wilful self-deception *Elizabeth would make no reply,* and immediately and in silence withdrew; *determined,* that if he persisted in considering her repeated refusals as flattering encouragement, *to apply to her father, whose negative might be uttered in such a manner as must be decisive, and whose behaviour at least could not be mistaken for the affectation and coquetry of an elegant female.*—JANE AUSTEN—*Pride and Prejudice.*

PRÉCIS

A Proposal

Mr. Collins, soon after breakfast, expressed to Mrs. Bennet the desire to speak privately with her daughter Elizabeth, who was also his cousin. The latter did not see the need for privacy, but on Mrs. Bennet's insistence agreed.

When they were left alone Mr. Collins proposed marriage, giving as his reasons that every clergyman in comfortable circumstances should set the example of matrimony to his flock; that it would add to his own happiness and that it was advised and recommended by his patroness, Lady Catherine de Bourgh, who advised him to select a gentlewoman who was both active and useful. These were his general reasons. The reason for choosing his cousin was that after her father's death he would inherit the Longbourn Estate, and he desired to minimise the loss to themselves. Furthermore, he had a very deep affection for Elizabeth.

She interrupted him with her refusal, but he would not take this as final, assuming that it was customary for young ladies to start off by rejecting the man they intended to accept. Elizabeth assured him of her sincerity. They would not make each other happy, and she thought that his patroness would find her ill-qualified for the situation. Collins said he would speak to her in highest terms of Elizabeth's modesty, economy and other amiable qualifications.

Elizabeth was unmoved; she said that Mr. Collins had satisfied his delicate feelings by his offer, and could now take the estate without self-reproach; he must consider the matter as finally settled. He again demurred, and hoped to receive a more favourable answer the next time. Elizabeth again repeated her refusal, but Mr. Collins still refused to take it seriously, as he considered that his hand and establishment were acceptable, while his situation in life, relations and connexions were highly favourable points. Also, Elizabeth with her small portion of £1,000 in the 4 per cents., might never, in spite of her attractions, receive another offer.

Elizabeth again assured him of her sincerity; she was not, as he presumed, keeping him in suspense—a practice which he deemed usual in the case of elegant females.

She was a rational creature speaking the truth from her heart. Mr. Collins, however, was still persuaded that she would accept him when his proposal was sanctioned by her parents.

Elizabeth, realising the futility of further remarks, withdrew and resolved to get her father to make her refusal decisive. His behaviour could not be mistaken for the caprice of an elegant female.

Précis of Technical and Commercial Matter

Certain types of technical and commercial data present their own problems in précis writing, and these we shall endeavour to elucidate in this chapter. Among the things which will be considered are Reports of Company Meetings, Acts of Parliament and Money Market Reports.

Reports of Company Meetings.—These are the speeches made, or rather read, by the chairmen of companies at the Annual General Meetings. Some are well-constructed; some are badly constructed, but in all cases it will be found that they tend to be verbose, and the essential points can be presented in a much shorter form. In making a précis of such reports it should be borne in mind that facts and figures are of much greater importance than the usual optimism as to the future which almost invariably takes up a large part of the speech. The main items which can with advantage be underlined at once for inclusion in the précis are :—

1. Results of past year's trading, and important revenue and capital developments.

2. Any further capital issued, and how the proceeds have been employed.

3. Amount of dividend and sums, if any, carried to reserve.

4. A brief summary of future prospects.

Example :

Make a précis of the following report :-

The Sixth Ordinary General Meeting of Telephone and General Trust, Limited, was held yesterday at *Incorporated Accountants' Hall, Victoria Embankment, W.C.*

Sir Alexander Rogers (the chairman) presided.

The Secretary (Mr. L. D. Bennett) having read the notice convening the meeting and the report of the auditors :

The Chairman said :—Gentlemen,—Before I make comment on the accounts I would recall my remarks of last year, when you were informed that it had been found necessary, owing to the expansion of our business, to segregate the auxiliary services given by the Trust to the companies in which it is directly interested, and *to form for this purpose a subsidiary company, by name, Telephone and Associated Services, Limited.*

This new company commenced its activities on February 28, 19—, and is working smoothly and satisfactorily.

RESULTS AND DIVIDENDS

You will find that the *gross income* of the Trust for the year is *£133,171 14s. 4d.,* and the *net profits at £84,548 7s. 8d.* show an appreciable increase of nearly 10 per cent. over last year's figure of £77,114 13s. 9d.

After deducting the *dividends on the 7 per cent. Cumulative Preference* shares *and* dividend of *7 per cent. on the Non-Cumulative Preferred Ordinary* shares, amounting in total to £56,893 13s. 9d., your directors recommend the payment of a *dividend of 8 per cent., less income-tax,* on the Ordinary shares, which is the same as for 19—, leaving the substantial balance of *£30,291 13s. 8d. to be carried forward,* representing just over 10 per cent. of the Ordinary share capital.

THE CAPITAL POSITION

On July 15 last *240,000 7 per cent. Cumulative Preference* shares, after being fully underwritten, were *issued* to the public at a price of *21s. per share.* The *proceeds* of the issue were used in *liquidation of loans* from bankers, in reducing loans from associated companies, in *financing affiliated companies, and in acquiring further investments.*

You will be pleased to note that the entire issue has been paid up in full. *An official quotation has been obtained* on all Preference shares in issue at December 31, 19—, both in London and in Liverpool Stock Exchanges.

Revenue Account

Dividends and interest representing only sums actually *received to* December 31, 19—, amount to *£121,441 11s. 11d.*, as against £100,590 8s., *an increase of £20,851 3s. 11d.* On the other hand, *fees and commissions* appear at *£11,707 4s. 5d.* as against £28,374 12s. 6d., *a decrease of £16,667 8s. 1d.*

A large portion of fees and commissions receivable was collected during 19— by *the new subsidiary services company*, thus *reducing the amount of* this item in the accounts now before you. Against this *a dividend* has been received from *the Services Company* for the period to December 31, 19—. *The net result is that our income from dividends and interests has been increased, whilst the income from fees, commissions, etc., has decreased.*

Interest on loans has been substantially *reduced* from £29,662 12s. 11d., to *£22,916 5s. 7d.*, largely owing to repayment of loans out of proceeds of the Preference share issue. *Management expenses* amount to *£18,932 13s. 2d.*, as against £17,865 11s. 9d. You would naturally have expected to see a reduction in the management expenses as a result of the work which has now been taken over by the subsidiary services company, but *expenses have increased owing to the increase in the volume of the Trust's normal business.*

Income-tax account is shown at £5,874 7s. 11d. This is merely an adjustment account, as all income is shown in our accounts gross.

As in former years, a certain amount of the business of the Trust has been carried out by means of short-term borrowings. The proceeds of the recent issue of Preference shares, however, have been applied partly in reduction of our short-term borrowings, which accounts *for the reduction of about £7,000 in interest payable.* On the other hand, the charge for Preference share dividend will be increased. I would mention that the cash proceeds of the share issue were received during the last few months of 19—, and have therefore been employed for a short period only in the accounts now before you. The net profit amounts to £84,548 7s. 8d., as against £77,114 13s. 9d. for 19—.

Note.—The most important figures are underlined.

PRÉCIS

Sixth Ordinary General Meeting of Telephone and General Trust Limited held at Incorporated Accountants' Hall, Victoria Embankment, W.C.

The Chairman, Sir Alexander Rogers, in opening his speech said that a subsidiary company had been formed to segregate the auxiliary services given by the Trust to other companies in which it was interested. This company was named Telephone and Associated Services Ltd., and commenced business on February 28th, 19...

Results and Dividends.—The net profit of £84,548 7s. 8d. showed an increase of nearly 10% over last year's figure. The gross income was £133,171 14s. 4d. After allowing 7% on Preference and Preferred Ordinary shares a dividend of 8% on the Ordinary shares was recommended, this leaving £30,291 13s. 8d. to be carried forward.

Capital Position.—240,000 7% Preference shares were underwritten and issued on July 15th, at 21s. each. The proceeds were used to liquidate and reduce loans, finance affiliated concerns and for investment. These were fully paid up and officially quoted, the proceeds being received towards the end of the year.

Revenue Account.—Dividends and Income received amounted to £121,441 11s. 11d., an increase of £20,851 3s. 11d. Fees and commissions received, at

£11,707 4s. 5d., showed a reduction of £16,667 8s. 1d., the decrease being largely due to the subsidiary company collecting items under this head, who had however paid a dividend to the Trust Co. The net result was an increase of dividends and interest and a decrease of fees, commissions, etc.

Loan interest was reduced by about £7,000 to £22,916 5s. 7d., but against this was an increased Preference dividend in respect of proceeds of the issue used to repay loans.

Management expenses were £18,932 13s. 2d., the increase being due to expansion of the Trust's normal business.

Acts of Parliament.—Many Acts of Parliament are notoriously complicated and even vague as to their precise meanings. To be understood at all they must be read and re-read and then analysed with great care. The ability to make précis of extracts from Statutes indicates a clear analytical mind and is well worth cultivating, since a student who can make a good précis of such a passage may rest assured that he need have no fear of the précis paper in his examination. An example is given below, although it will be found that care and practice are the main essentials in writing this form of précis.

Example :

If, on an application made by any individual, either at the time of making his return for the purposes of super-tax for any year or within the time limited for appealing against the assessment upon him to super-tax for that year, the applicant proves to the satisfaction of the Special Commissioners that, in consequence of the sale or transfer to him of any assets, the amount of super-tax payable by him for that year exceeds by more than ten per cent. the amount of the super-tax which would have been payable by him for that year if the income from those assets and from any assets sold or transferred by him were deemed to have accrued from day to day, then, for the purposes of any assessment to super-tax in the case of that individual for that year, the income from all such assets as aforesaid shall be deemed to have accrued from day to day and to have been received by him as and when it is deemed to have accrued.

PRÉCIS

Relief from Super-tax

Where an applicant satisfies the Special Commissioners, within the time allowed for appeals against super-tax assessments, that assets transferred to him caused his assessment to exceed by over 10% the amount which would have been payable if the income therefrom was taken as accruing from day to day, such income is to be taken as so accruing and to have been received when deemed to have accrued.

Market Reports. The chief difficulty in making précis of these is that they are already in précis form, and to achieve further condensation is by no means an easy matter. The following example will show how such a question should be tackled.

Example :

In spite of the absence of Treasury Bill maturities on Saturday, short credit was in abundant supply throughout the session. During the opening hours the usual rate for loans was $1\frac{3}{4}$ per cent. to 2 per cent., but towards the close there were large sums on offer at $1\frac{1}{2}$ per cent. Indeed, in some cases balances had to be left unemployed. A little bank buying of short maturities was reported.

Précis

Although Treasury maturities were absent on Saturday, short credit was abundant. The usual rate for loans was $1\frac{3}{4}\%$ to 2%, easing later to $1\frac{1}{2}\%$, at which rate all was not taken. Banks bought a few short bills.

Miscellaneous Points. It occasionally happens that examination candidates are required to give the substance of a passage in their own words in a shorter form than the original. In such a case, the ordinary rules for précis writing should be followed, except that, strictly speaking, it is not essential to alter the tense to the past, or e.g., to substitute the pronoun *he* for *I* as would be done in a précis proper. It is, however, safer to follow the rules of précis fairly closely, unless this is impracticable. If we are asked to give the substance of a passage containing dialect or old English phraseology, this should be changed into modern and good English.

EXAMPLES FOR PRÉCIS:

1. On Monday the Fourteenth of October 1793, a Cause is pending in the Palais de Justice, in the new Revolutionary Court, such as these old stone-walls never witnessed : the Trial of Marie-Antoinette. The once brightest of Queens, now tarnished, defaced, forsaken, stands here at Fouquier-Tinville's Judgement-bar; answering for her life. The Indictment was delivered her last night. To such changes of human fortune what words are adequate ? Silence alone is adequate.

There are few Printed things one meets with of such tragic, almost ghastly, significance as those bald Pages of the *Bulletin du Tribunal Révolutionnaire*, which bear title, *Trial of the Widow Capet*. Dim, dim, as if in disastrous eclipse; like the pale kingdom of Dis ! Plutonic Judges,

Plutonic Tinville; encircled, nine times, with Styx and Lethe, with Fire-Phlegethon and Cocytus named of Lamentation ! The very witnesses summoned are like Ghosts : exculpatory, inculpatory, they themselves are all hovering over death and doom ; they are known, in our imagination, as the prey of the Guillotine. Tall *ci-devant* Count d'Estaing, anxious to show himself Patriot, cannot escape ; nor Bailly, who, when asked If he knows the Accused, answers with a reverent inclination towards her, " Ah, yes, I know Madame." Ex-Patriots are here, sharply dealt with, as Procureur Manuel ; Ex-Ministers, shorn of their splendour. We have cold Aristocratic impassivity, faithful to itself even in Tartarus ; rabid stupidity, of Patriot Corporals, Patriot Washerwomen, who have much to say of Plots, Treasons, August Tenth, old Insurrection of Women. For all now has become a crime in her who has *lost.*

Marie-Antoinette, in this her utter abandonment, and hour of extreme need, is not wanting to herself, the imperial woman. Her look, they say, as that hideous Indictment was reading, continued calm ; " she was sometimes observed moving her fingers, as when one plays on the piano." You discern, not without interest, across that dim Revolutionary Bulletin itself, how she bears herself queenlike. Her answers are prompt, clear, often of Laconic brevity ; resolution, which has grown contemptuous without ceasing to be dignified, veils itself in calm words. " You persist, then, in denial ? "—" My plan is not denial : it is the truth I have said, and I persist in that." Scandalous Hébert has borne his testimony as to many things : as to one thing, concerning Marie-Antoinette and her little Son,— wherewith Human Speech had better not farther be soiled. She has answered Hébert ; a Juryman begs to observe that she has not answered as to *this*. " I have not answered," she exclaims with noble emotion, " because Nature refuses to answer such a charge brought against a Mother. I appeal to all the Mothers that are here." Robespierre, when he heard of it, broke out into something almost like swearing at the brutish blockheadism of this Hébert ; on whose foul head his foul lie has recoiled. At four o'clock on Wednesday morning, after two days and two nights of interrogating, jury-charging, and other darkening of counsel, the result comes out : sentence of Death. " Have you anything to say ? " The Accused shook her head, without speech. Night's candles are burning out; and with her too Time is finishing, and it will be Eternity and Day. This Hall of Tinville's is dark, ill-lighted except where she stands. Silently she withdraws from it, to die.

Two Processions, or Royal Progresses, three-and-twenty years apart, have often struck us with a strange feeling of contrast. The first is of a beautiful Archduchess and Dauphiness, quitting her Mother's City, at the age of Fifteen; towards hopes such as no other Daughter of Eve then had : " On the morrow," says Weber an eye-witness, " the Dauphiness left Vienna. The whole city crowded out; at first with a sorrow which was silent. She appeared : you saw her sunk back into her carriage; her face bathed in tears; hiding her eyes now with her hand-kerchief, now with her hands; several times putting out her head to see yet again this Palace of her Fathers, whither she was to return no more. She motioned her regret, her gratitude to the good Nation, which was crowding here to bid her farewell. Then arose not only tears; but piercing cries, on all sides. Men and women alike abandoned themselves to such expression of their sorrow. It was an audible sound of wail, in the streets and avenues of Vienna. The last Courier that followed her disappeared, and the crowd melted away."

The young imperial Maiden of Fifteen has now become a worn discrowned Widow of Thirty-eight; grey before her time : this is the last Procession : " Few minutes after the Trial ended, the drums were beating to arms in all Sections; at sunrise the armed force was on foot, cannons getting placed at the extremities of the Bridges, in the Squares, Crossways, all along from the Palais de Justice to the Place de la Révolution. By ten o'clock, numerous patrols were circulating in the Streets; thirty thousand foot and horse drawn up under arms. At eleven, Marie-Antoinette was brought out. She had on an undress of *piqué blanc*: she was led to the place of execution, in the same manner as an ordinary criminal; bound, on a Cart; accompanied by a Constitutional Priest in Lay dress; escorted by numerous detachments of infantry and cavalry. These, and the double row of troops all along her road, she appeared to regard with indifference. On her countenance there was visible neither abashment nor pride. To the cries of *Vive la République* and *Down with Tyranny*, which attended her all the way, she seemed to pay no heed. She spoke little to her Confessor. The tricolor Streamers on the housetops occupied her attention, in the Streets du Roule and Saint-Honoré; she also noticed the Inscriptions on the house-fronts. On reaching the Place de la Révolution, her looks turned towards the *Jardin National*, whilom Tuileries; her face at that moment gave signs of lively emotion. She mounted the Scaffold with courage enough; at a quarter past Twelve, her head fell; the Executioner showed it to the people, amid universal long-continued cries of *Vive la République*."

THOMAS CARLYLE.—*History of the French Revolution.*

2. Now came her trial. This trial, moving of course under English influence, was conducted in chief by the Bishop of Beauvais. He was a Frenchman, sold to English interests, and hoping, by favour of the English leaders, to reach the highest preferment. *Bishop that art, Archbishop that shalt be, Cardinal that mayest be,* were the words that sounded continually in his ear; and doubtless a whisper of visions still higher, of a triple crown, and feet upon the necks of kings, sometimes stole into his heart. M. Michelet is anxious to keep us in mind that this bishop was but an agent of the English. True. But it does not better the case for his countryman—that, being an accomplice in the crime, making himself the leader in the persecution against the helpless girl, he was willing to be all this in the spirit, and with the conscious vileness of a cat's-paw. Never from the foundations of the earth was there such a trial as this, if it were laid open in all its beauty of defence, and all its hellishness of attack. Oh, child of France! shepherdess, peasant girl! trodden under foot by all around thee, how I honour thy flashing intellect, quick as God's lightning, and true as God's lightning to its mark, that ran before France and laggard Europe by many a century, confounding the malice of the ensnarer, and making dumb

the oracles of falsehood ! Is it not scandalous, is it not humiliating to civilization, that, even at this day, France exhibits the horrid spectacle of judges examining the prisoner against himself; seducing him, by fraud, into treacherous conclusions against his own head; using the terrors of their power for extorting confessions from the frailty of hope; nay (which is worse), using the blandishments of condescension and snaky kindness for thawing into compliances of gratitude those whom they had failed to freeze into terror ? Wicked judges ! Barbarian jurisprudence ! that, sitting in your own conceit on the summits of social wisdom, have yet failed to learn the first principles of criminal justice; sit ye humbly and with docility at the feet of this girl from Domrémy, that tore your webs of cruelty into shreds and dust. " Would you examine me as a witness against myself ? " was the question by which many times she defied their arts. Continually she showed that their interrogations were irrelevant to any business before the court, or that entered into the ridiculous charges against her. General questions were proposed to her on points of casuistical divinity; two-edged questions, which not one of themselves could have answered, without, on the one side, landing himself in heresy (as then interpreted), or, on the other, in some presumptuous expression of self-esteem. Next came a wretched Dominican, that pressed her with an objection, which, if applied to the Bible, would tax every one of its miracles with unsoundness. The monk had the excuse of never having read the Bible. M. Michelet has no such excuse; and it makes one blush for him, as a philosopher, to find him describing such an argument as " weighty," whereas it is but a varied expression of rude Mahometan metaphysics. Her answer to this, if there were room to place the whole in a clear light, was as shattering as it was rapid. Another thought to entrap her by asking what language the angelic visitors of her solitude had talked; as though heavenly counsels could want polyglot interpreters for every word, or that God needed language at all in whispering thoughts to a human heart. Then came a worse devil, who asked her whether the archangel Michael had appeared naked. Not comprehending the vile insinuation, Joanna, whose poverty suggested to her simplicity that it might be the *costliness* of suitable robes which caused the demur, asked them if they fancied God, who clothed the flowers of the valleys, unable to find raiment for his servants. The answer of Joanna moves a smile of tenderness, but the disappointment of her judges makes one laugh exultingly. Others succeeded by troops, who upbraided her with leaving her father; as if that greater Father, whom she believed herself to have been serving, did not retain the power of dispensing with his own rules, or had not said, that for a less cause than martyrdom, man and woman should leave both father and mother.

On Easter Sunday, when the trial had been long proceeding, the poor girl fell so ill as to cause a belief that she had been poisoned. It was not poison. Nobody had any interest in hastening a death so certain. M. Michelet, whose sympathies with all feelings are so quick, that one would gladly see them always as justly directed, reads the case most truly. Joanna had a twofold malady. She was visited by a paroxysm of the complaint called *home-sickness*; the cruel nature of her imprisonment, and its length, could not but point her solitary thoughts, in darkness and in chains (for chained she was), to Domrémy. And the season, which was the most heavenly period of the spring, added stings to this yearning. That was one of her maladies —*nostalgia*, as medicine calls it; the other was weariness and exhaustion from daily combats with malice. She saw that everybody hated her, and thirsted for her blood; nay, many kind-hearted creatures that would have pitied her profoundly, as regarded all political charges, had their natural feelings warped by the belief that she had dealings with fiendish powers. She knew she was to die; that was *not* the misery : the misery was, that this consummation could not be reached without so much intermediate strife, as if she were contending for some chance (where chance was none) of happiness, or were dreaming for a moment of escaping the inevitable. Why, then, *did* she contend ? Knowing that she would reap nothing from answering her persecutors, why did she not retire by silence from the superfluous contest ? It was because her quick and eager loyalty to truth would not suffer her to see it darkened by frauds, which *she* could expose, but others, even of candid listeners, perhaps, could not; it was through that imperishable grandeur of soul, which taught her to submit meekly and without a struggle to her punishment, but taught her *not* to submit—no, not for a moment—to calumny as to facts, or to misconstruction as to motives. Besides, there were secretaries all around the court taking down her words. That was meant for no good to *her* But the end does not always correspond to the meaning. And Joanna might say to herself—these words that will be used against me to-morrow and the next day, perhaps in some nobler generation may rise again for my justification. Yes, Joanna, they *are* rising even now in Paris, and for more than justification.

THOMAS DE QUINCEY.—Joan of Arc.

3. *Young Fashion.* Come, pay the waterman, and take the portmantle.

Lory. Faith, sir, I think the waterman had as good take the portmantle, and pay himself.

Young Fashion. Why, sure there's something left in't.

Lory. But a solitary old waistcoat, upon my honour, sir.

Young Fashion. Why, what's become of the blue coat, sirrah?

Lory. Sir, 'twas eaten at Gravesend; the reckoning came to thirty shillings, and your privy purse was worth but two half-crowns.

Young Fashion. 'Tis very well.

Waterman. Pray, master, will you please to dispatch me?

Young Fashion. Ay, here, a—Canst thou change me a guinea?

Lory [*aside*]. Good.

Waterman. Change a guinea, master! Ha, ha, your honour's pleas'd to compliment.

Young Fashion. I'gad I don't know how I shall pay thee then, for I have nothing but gold about me.

Lory [*aside*]. Hum, hum.

Young Fashion. What dost thou expect, friend?

Waterman. Why, master, so far against wind and tide, is richly worth half a piece.

Young Fashion. Why, faith, I think thou art a good conscionable fellow. I'gad, I begin to have so good an opinion of thy honesty, I care not if I leave my portmantle with thee, till I send thee thy money.

Waterman. Ha! God bless your honour; I should be as willing to trust you, master, but that you are, as a man may say, a stranger to me, and these are nimble times; there are a great many sharpers stirring. [*Taking up the portmantle.*] Well, master, when your worship sends the money, your portmantle shall be forthcoming; my name's Tugg, my wife keeps a brandy-shop in Drab-Alley at Wapping.

Young Fashion. Very well; I'll send for 't to-morrow.

[*Exit* Waterman.

Lory. So——Now, sir, I hope you'll own yourself a happy man, you have outliv'd all your cares.

Young Fashion. How so, sir?

Lory. Why, you have nothing left to take care of.

Young Fashion. Yes, sirrah, I have myself and you to take care of still.

Lory. Sir, if you could but prevail with somebody else to do that for you, I fancy we might both fare the better for 't.

Young Fashion. Why, if thou canst tell me where to apply myself, I have at present so little money, and so much humility about me, I don't know but I may follow a fool's advice.

Lory. Why then, sir, your fool advises you to lay aside all animosity, and apply to Sir Novelty, your elder brother.

Young Fashion. Damn my elder brother.

Lory. With all my heart; but get him to redeem your annuity, however.

Young Fashion. My annuity! 'Sdeath, he's such a dog, he would not give his powder-puff to redeem my soul.

Lory. Look you, sir, you must wheedle him, or you must starve.

Young Fashion. Look you, sir, I will neither wheedle him, nor starve.

Lory. Why? what will you do then?

L

Young Fashion. I'll go into the army.

Lory. You can't take the oaths; you are a Jacobite.

Young Fashion. Thou may'st as well say I can't take orders because I'm an atheist.

Lory. Sir, I ask your pardon; I find I did not know the strength of your conscience, so well as I did the weakness of your purse.

Young Fashion. Methinks, sir, a person of your experience should have known, that the strength of the conscience proceeds from the weakness of the purse.

Lory. Sir, I am very glad to find you have a conscience able to take care of us, let it proceed from what it will; but I desire you'll please to consider, that the army alone will be but a scanty maintenance for a person of your generosity (at least as rents now are paid); I shall see you stand in damnable need of some auxiliary guineas for your *menus plaisirs*; I will therefore turn fool once more for your service, and advise you to go directly to your brother.

Young Fashion. Art thou then so impregnable a blockhead, to believe he'll help me with a farthing?

Lory. Not if you treat him *de haut en bas*, as you use to do.

Young Fashion. Why, how would'st have me treat him?

Lory. Like a trout, tickle him.

Young Fashion. I can't flatter——

Lory. Can you starve?

Young Fashion. Yes——

Lory. I can't; Goodbye t'ye, sir——

[*Going.*

Young Fashion. Stay, thou wilt distract me. What would'st thou have me to say to him?

Lory. Say nothing to him, apply yourself to his favourites; speak to his periwig, his cravat, his feather, his snuffbox, and when you are well with them—desire him to lend you a thousand pounds. I'll engage you prosper.

Young Fashion. 'Sdeath and Furies! Why was that coxcomb thrust into the world before me? O Fortune—Fortune—thou art a bitch, by Gad——

[*Exeunt.*

SIR JOHN VANBRUGH.—*The Relapse.*

4. Much about the same time I walked out into the
fields towards Bow; for I had a great mind to see how
things were managed in the river and among the ships;
and as I had some concern in shipping, I had a notion
that it had been one of the best ways of securing one's self
from the infection to have retired into a ship; and musing
how to satisfy my curiosity in that point, I turned away
over the fields from Bow to Bromley, and down to Black-
wall to the stairs, which are there for landing or taking
water.

Here I saw a poor man walking on the bank, or sea-wall,
as they call it, by himself. I walked a while also about,
seeing the houses all shut up; at last I fell into some talk,
at a distance, with this poor man; first I asked him how
people did thereabouts. "Alas, sir!" says he, "almost
all desolate; all dead or sick. Here are very few families
in this part, or in that village," pointing at Poplar, "where
half of them are not dead already, and the rest sick." Then
he pointed to one house. "There they are all dead," said
he, "and the house stands open; nobody dares go into it.
A poor thief," says he, "ventured in to steal something,
but he paid dear for his theft, for he was carried to the
churchyard too last night." Then he pointed to several
other houses. "There," says he, "they are all dead, the
man and his wife, and five children. There," says he,
"they are shut up; you see a watchman at the door";
and so of other houses. "Why," says I, "what do you
here all alone?" "Why," says he, "I am a poor, desolate
man; it has pleased God I am not yet visited, though my
family is, and one of my children dead." "How do you
mean, then," said I, "that you are not visited?" "Why,"
says he, "that's my house," pointing to a very little, low-
boarded house, "and there my poor wife and two children
live," said he, "if they may be said to live, for my wife
and one of the children are visited, but I do not come at
them." And with that word I saw the tears run very
plentifully down his face; and so they did down mine too,
I assure you.

But said I, "Why do you not come at them? How can
you abandon your own flesh and blood?" "Oh, sir,"
says he, "the Lord forbid! I do not abandon them; I

work for them as much as I am able; and, blessed be the
Lord, I keep them from want; " and with that I observed
he lifted up his eyes to heaven, with a countenance that
presently told me I had happened on a man that was no
hypocrite, but a serious, religious, good man, and his
ejaculation was an expression of thankfulness that, in
such a condition as he was in, he should be able to say
his family did not want. " Well," says I, " honest man,
that is a great mercy as things go now with the poor.
But how do you live, then, and how are you kept from
the dreadful calamity that is now upon us all? " " Why,
sir," says he, " I am a waterman, and there's my boat,"
says he, " and the boat serves me for a house. I work in
it in the day, and I sleep in it in the night; and what J
get I lay down upon that stone," says he, showing me a
broad stone on the other side of the street, a good way
from his house; " and then," says he, " I halloo, and call
to them till I make them hear; and they come and fetch
it."

" Well, friend," says I, " but how can you get any
money as a waterman? Does anybody go by water these
times? " " Yes, sir," says he, " in the way I am employed
there does. Do you see there," says he, " five ships lie at
anchor," pointing down the river a good way below the
town, " and do you see," says he, " eight or ten ships lie
at the chain there, and at anchor yonder," pointing above
the town. " All those ships have families on board, of
their merchants and owners, and such-like, who have locked
themselves up and live on board, close shut in, for fear of
the infection; and I tend on them to fetch things for
them, carry letters, and do what is absolutely necessary,
that they may not be obliged to come on shore; and
every night I fasten my boat on board one of the ship's
boats, and there I sleep by myself, and, blessed be God,
I am preserved hitherto."

" Well," said I, " friend, but will they let you come on
board after you have been on shore here, when this is such
a terrible place, and so infected as it is? "

" Why, as to that," said he, " I very seldom go up the
ship-side, but deliver what I bring to their boat, or lie by
the side, and they hoist it on board. If I did, I think

they are in no danger from me, for I never go into any house on shore, or touch anybody, no, not of my own family; but I fetch provisions for them."

"Nay," says I, "but that may be worse, for you must have those provisions of somebody or other; and since all this part of the town is so infected, it is dangerous so much as to speak with anybody, for this village," said I, "is, as it were, the beginning of London, though it be at some distance from it."

"That is true," added he; "but you do not understand me right; I do not buy provisions for them here. I row up to Greenwich and buy fresh meat there, and sometimes I row down the river to Woolwich and buy there; then I go to single farm-houses on the Kentish side, where I am known, and buy fowls and eggs and butter, and bring to the ships, as they direct me, sometimes one, sometimes the other. I seldom come on shore here, and I came now only to call to my wife and hear how my little family do, and give them a little money, which I received last night."

"Poor man!" said I; "and how much hast thou gotten for them?"

"I have gotten four shillings," said he, "which is a great sum, as things go now with poor men; but they have given me a bag of bread too, and a salt fish and some flesh; so all helps out."

"Well," said I, "and have you given it them yet?"

"No," said he, "but I have called, and my wife has answered that she cannot come out yet, but in half-an-hour she hopes to come, and I am waiting for her. Poor woman!" says he, "she is brought sadly down. She has a swelling, and it is broke, and I hope she will recover; but I fear the child will die, but it is the Lord——"

Here he stopped, and wept very much.

"Well, honest friend," said I, "thou hast a sure Comforter, if thou hast brought thyself to be resigned to the will of God; He is dealing with us all in judgment."

"Oh, sir!" says he, "it is infinite mercy if any of us are spared, and who am I to repine!"

"Sayest thou so?" said I, "and how much less is my faith than thine?" And here my heart smote me, suggesting how much better this poor man's foundation was

on which he stayed in the danger than mine; that he had
nowhere to fly; that he had a family to bind him to attend-
ance, which I had not; and mine was mere presumption.
his a true dependence, and a courage resting on God; and
yet that he used all possible caution for his safety.

I turned a little way from the man while these thoughts
engaged me, for, indeed, I could no more refrain from tears
than he.

At length, after some further talk, the poor woman
opened the door and called, " Robert, Robert." He
answered, and bid her stay a few moments and he would
come; so he ran down the common stairs to his boat and
fetched up a sack, in which was the provisions he had
brought from the ships; and when he returned he hallooed
again. Then he went to the great stone which he showed
me and emptied the sack, and laid all out, everything by
themselves, and then retired; and his wife came with a
little boy to fetch them away, and he called and said such
a captain had sent such a thing, and such a captain such
a thing, and at the end adds, " God has sent it all; give
thanks to Him." When the poor woman had taken up
all, she was so weak she could not carry it at once in, though
the weight was not much, so she left the biscuit, which
was in a little bag, and left a little boy to watch it till she
came again.

" Well, but," says I to him, " did you leave her the four
shillings too, which you said was your week's pay ? "

" Yes, yes," says he; " you shall hear her own it." So
he calls again, " Rachel, Rachel," which, it seems, was her
name, " did you take up the money ? " " Yes," said she.
" How much was it ? " said he. " Four shillings and a
groat," said she. " Well, well," says he, " the Lord keep
you all; " and so he turned to go away.

As I could not refrain contributing tears to this man's
story, so neither could I refrain my charity for his assistance; so I called him, " Hark thee, friend," said I, " come
hither, for I believe thou art in health, that I may venture
thee; " so I pulled out my hand, which was in my pocket
before, " Here," says I, " go and call thy Rachel once
more, and give her a little more comfort from me. God
will never forsake a family that trust in Him as thou dost."

So I gave him four other shillings, and bade him go lay them on the stone and call his wife.

I have not words to express the poor man's thankfulness, neither could he express it himself but by tears running down his face. He called his wife, and told her God had moved the heart of a stranger, upon hearing their condition, to give them all that money, and a great deal more such as that he said to her. The woman, too, made signs of the like thankfulness, as well to Heaven as to me, and joyfully picked it up; and I parted with no money all that year that I thought better bestowed.

DANIEL DEFOE.—*A Journal of the Plague Year.*

5. We sailed from Peru (where we had continued by the space of one whole year), for China and Japan, by the South Sea, taking with us victuals for twelve months; and had good winds from the east, though soft and weak, for five months' space and more. But then the wind came about, and settled in the west for many days, so as we could make little or no way, and were sometimes in purpose to turn back. But then again there arose strong and great winds from the south, with a point east; which carried us up, for all that we could do, towards the north: by which time our victuals failed us, though we had made good spare of them. So that finding ourselves, in the midst of the greatest wilderness of waters in the world, without victual, we gave ourselves for lost men, and prepared for death. Yet we did lift up our hearts and voices to God above, who " showeth His wonders in the deep "; beseeching Him of His mercy, that as in the beginning He discovered the face of the deep, and brought forth dry land, so He would now discover land to us, that we might not perish. And it came to pass that the next day about evening we saw within a kenning before us, towards the north, as it were thick clouds, which did put us in some hope of land; knowing how that part of the South Sea was utterly unknown; and might have islands or continents that hitherto were not come to light. Wherefore we bent our course thither, where we saw the appearance of land, all that night; and in the dawning of the next day, we might plainly discern that it was a land, flat to our sight

and full of boscage; which made it show the more dark. And after an hour and a half's sailing, we entered into a good haven, being the port of a fair city : not great, indeed, but well built, and that gave a pleasant view from the sea. And we thinking every minute long till we were on land, came close to the shore and offered to land. But straightways we saw divers of the people, with bastons in their hands, as it were, forbidding us to land : yet without any cries or fierceness, but only as warning us off, by signs that they made. Whereupon being not a little discomforted, we were advising with ourselves what we should do. During which time there made forth to us a small boat, with about eight persons in it, whereof one of them had in his hand a tipstaff of a yellow cane, tipped at both ends with blue, who came aboard our ship, without any show of distrust at all. And when he saw one of our number present himself somewhat afore the rest, he drew forth a little scroll of parchment (somewhat yellower than our parchment, and shining like the leaves of writing tables, but otherwise soft and flexible), and delivered it to our foremost man. In which scroll were written in ancient Hebrew, and in ancient Greek, and in good Latin of the school, and in Spanish, these words : " Land ye not, none of you, and provide to be gone from this coast within sixteen days, except you have further time given you. Meanwhile, if you want fresh water, or victual, or help for your sick, or that your ship needeth repair, write down your wants, and you shall have that which belongeth to mercy." This scroll was signed with a stamp of cherubim's wings, not spread, but hanging downwards; and by them a cross. This being delivered, the officer returned, and left only a servant with us to receive our answer. Consulting hereupon amongst ourselves, we were much perplexed. The denial of landing, and hasty warning us away, troubled us much; on the other side, to find that the people had languages, and were so full of humanity, did comfort us not a little. And above all, the sign of the Cross to that instrument, was to us a great rejoicing, and as it were a certain presage of good. Our answer was in the Spanish tongue, " That for our ship, it was well; for we had rather met with calms, and contrary winds, than any tempests.

For our sick, they were many, and in very ill case; so that if they were not permitted to land, they ran danger of their lives." Our other wants we set down in particular; adding, "That we had some little store of merchandise, which, if it pleased them to deal for, it might supply our wants, without being chargeable unto them." We offered some reward in pistolets unto the servant, and a piece of crimson velvet to be presented to the officer : but the servant took them not, nor would scarce look upon them; and so left us, and went back in another little boat, which was sent for him.

About three hours after we had dispatched our answer there came towards us a person (as it seemed) of place. He had on him a gown with wide sleeves, of a kind of water chamolet, of an excellent azure colour, far more glossy than ours : his under apparel was green, and so was his hat, being in the form of a turban, daintily made, and not so huge as the Turkish turbans; and the locks of his hair came down below the brims of it. A reverend man was he to behold. He came in a boat, gilt in some part of it, with four persons more only in that boat; and was followed by another boat, wherein were some twenty. When he was come within a flight-shot of our ship, signs were made to us that we should send forth some to meet him upon the water; which we presently did in our ship-boat, sending the principal man amongst us save one, and four of our number with him. When we were come within six yards of their boat, they called to us to stay, and not to approach further, which we did. And thereupon the man, whom I before described, stood up, and with a loud voice, in Spanish, asked, "Are ye Christians?" We answered, "We were"; fearing the less, because of the Cross we had seen in the subscription. At which answer the said person lifted up his right hand towards Heaven, and drew it softly to his mouth (which is the gesture they use, when they thank God), and then said : "If ye will swear, all of you, by the merits of the Saviour, that ye are no pirates, nor have shed blood, lawfully nor unlawfully, within forty days past, you may have licence to come on land." We said, "We were all ready to take that oath." Whereupon one of those that were with him, being (as it seemed) a notary, made an entry of this act. Which done, another of the attendants of the great person, which was with him in the same boat, after his lord had spoken a little to him, said aloud : " My lord would have you know, that it is not of pride, or greatness, that he cometh not aboard your ship : but for that, in your answer, you declare that you have many sick amongst you, he was warned by the Conservator of Health of the city that he should keep a distance." We bowed ourselves towards him, and answered, " We were his humble servants ; and accounted for great honour and singular humanity towards us, that which was already done : but hoped well, that the nature of the sickness of our men was not infectious." So he returned ; and a while after came the notary to us aboard our ship, holding in his hand a fruit of that country, like an orange, but of colour between orange-tawny and scarlet ; which cast a most excellent odour. He used it (as it seemeth) for a preservative against infection. He gave us our oath, " By the name of Jesus, and His merits " : and after told us, that the next day, by six of the clock in the morning, we should be sent to, and brought to the Strangers' House (so he called it), where we should be accommodated of things, both for our whole and for our sick. So he left us, and when we offered him some pistolets, he smiling said, " He must not be twice paid for one labour " ; meaning (as I take it), that he had salary sufficient of the State for his service. For (as I after learned) they call an officer that taketh rewards, twice-paid.

FRANCIS BACON.—*New Atlantis.*

6. Read the story given below, and then answer the following questions.

QUESTION 1—Write in your own words a summary of the story. If you use more than 175 words you will lose marks. State at the foot of your answer the number of words you have used.

QUESTION 2—Do you approve of such a method of making a guilty man confess ? Give reasons.

QUESTION 3—Explain the following words or phrases as used in the passage :—
alibi, the third degree, wall-eyed, hamstrung.

The Fourth Degree

The Deputy Commissioner of Jedpur, Cedric Marshall, C.S.I., and the Superintendent of the police, Major Stanley, sat out on the veranda in the warm dusk, chatting over their whiskies and cheroots.

" It's just my cursed luck, Stanley," said the Deputy Commissioner, " to land up at this one-eyed hole just when someone has thought fit to upset the local farmers by hacking their cattle about. And unless something's done quickly, there's going to be some trouble. It's up to your people to fix the cattle-maimer. What have they done about it ? "

" Done ? " The police officer professed to be astonished. " My dear fellow, you have had the results of their zeal in front of you to-day. Five suspects. Five, not a miserable *one*—and the very knife the maimer used."

" Oh, talk sense ! " grunted the other. " How can I be expected to sort out which of the five is the one ? Your people can't prove whose knife it is. It's a common pattern . . ."

" But Solomon . . ."

" I'm not Solomon. I'm a thoroughly fed-up Indian Civilian who'll be glad to retire on pension and settle down in Blighty, far away from this sun-baked, mosquito-ridden country ! "

" Better make it ten grains of quinine to-night," kindly suggested Stanley. " I was going to remark that Solomon . . ."

" Or the Caliph of Baghdad," again interrupted the Deputy Commissioner, " would hit the right nail on the head by cracking the whole five. There's something to be said for that old-fashioned method of keeping law and order. In these enlightened days, though, we have a rigid criminal code which insists that only the guilty suffer."

" I see your difficulty," said the Major. " My local officer has been over-zealous. Five suspects is rather a lot, an embarrassment of choice, eh ? It just shows what a great deal he thinks of the magistrate-sahib ; a sort of test for your wisdom."

" Chuck it ! " The Deputy Commissioner laughed in

spite of himself. " You know as well as I it's sheer incompetence. Mind you, he's got the fellow right enough—among them. But guilt has got to be demonstrated. I can't punish the whole crowd for what is unquestionably the work of one man."

Major Stanley stared thoughtfully into the night.

" Yes—of course," he said at last, " it's that wall-eyed, pock-marked worm, Mahmoud Ali."

" And if there's anything to choose among their beautifully got-up alibis, his is a flawless gem—too damned flawless ! He was always, apparently, among his pals, the night an outrage took place."

" I think," said the Major, emptying his glass and rising, " I'll have a shot at getting a confession from him."

" I know my India," said the other. " You could put him on the rack or sear him through and through with hot needles—and he'll remain mum. No, my boy. You've got to find proofs—and the affair must be settled quickly, or we'll have a fine old riot between the Hindu and Mahommedan."

" I've no intention of trying the third degree, Marshall—that isn't done. But I know something of the native mind and its reactions to inexplicable things. I call my method the Fourth Degree. Take your quinine and turn in. I've an idea you'll be able to discharge four of the crew to-morrow. Good night, old man."

There was a ripple of excitement next morning when it was announced by the clerk of the court that His Excellency would first deal with the cattle-maiming affair which had been adjourned; and Major Stanley, who was seated by him, nodded to his native officer to march the arrested men in.

The five suspects filed in under escort and salaamed together like automatons. The Major ran his eye along them, though they rested a little longer on the fourth—him with the wall-eye and pock-marked skin—than on any of the others.

With no further formality, as it was an adjourned case, Cedric Marshall addressed the accused :

" Undoubtedly one of you is guilty of this detestable crime : the evidence is quite clear that . . ."

"Highness," pleaded one, "may my right hand wither if . . ."

"Never, O Great One," cried another, "have I harmed man or beast . . ."

"And every night the farmers' cattle were hamstrung," a third chimed in, "I was with my brother-in-law . . ."

"Peace!" The peremptory command came from the police-sahib, who rose and stepped down from the daïs in front of the five men. "Hold out your knife-hands with the palm upwards," he ordered them. "Maybe I shall see the blood-mark of guilt on that of the evil-doer!"

Humbly they obeyed; but the wall-eyed Mahmoud Ali first apprehensively glanced at his palm—and the Major threw a quiet glance back at his friend, the judge. The police escort and all those near by craned forward to satisfy their curiosity.

Evidently, though, not one palm showed any such stain. The police-sahib shook his head dubiously, but spoke to his native subordinate : "Bring me the knife you found, the other night, in one of the maimed cattle."

The blood-stained exhibit was in the court and was handed to him. In a tense, expectant silence he gravely, as if carrying out a ritual, placed it carefully in the centre of a small table standing in front of the daïs; then he beckoned to the first of the suspects. Mahommed Azim shuffled forward.

"Hold thy knife-hand above this knife, this way!" The Major took the open brown hand and, turning it palm downward, drew it forward so that it was immediately over, a foot or two above, the knife; he stepped away, waited a few moments, then spoke again : "Now show thy hand to the magistrate-sahib. If the stain is there, thou art the guilty one!"

Mahommed Azim withdrew his hand, looked at it, then triumphantly held it up for the judge and all to see.

"Discharged!" said Marshall sahib curtly—and the man melted back into a little crowd of his own friends and relatives.

"Ali Khan, come here!" said Major Stanley to the next suspect, and drew his hand, also, into the proper position above the knife before stepping back.

Ali Khan held his hand there a moment, turned it over, looked at the palm, then held it up for public view.

" Discharged ! " said the judge. " Next ! "

The next man also survived the curious ordeal. The fourth was the wall-eyed, pock-marked Mahmoud Ali, who was already visibly paling. His knife-hand was trembling when the police-sahib drew it into position above the knife and turned it palm downward ; and it could be seen shaking when the officer stepped away.

" Now," ordered Major Stanley, " hold it up so that the magistrate-sahib and all may see whether thou are guiltless or not ! "

Mahmoud Ali slowly withdrew his shaking hand and turned it over.

" *Allah ! Allah ! Allah !* "

The exclamations burst from a dozen lips—for everyone could see, clear and distinct in the centre of his palm, a crimson stain that had not been there before !

Mahmoud Ali, himself, was staring at it. Suddenly he cast himself down on the mud floor in front of the magistrate.

" O Cadi," he wailed, " thou and police-sahib are all-seeing and all-wise. Have mercy. 'Tis I who slashed the farmers' cattle. That is my knife. *It* knew ! "

" Quite simple, Marshall ! " explained Major Stanley when the session was over and they were alone. " You remember I went to the trouble, myself, of placing each man's hand in position. Well, it was only natural for my thumb to touch his palm ; but in every case except that of the man we were both morally certain of, it was only with the extreme tip. In his case, though, the full ball of my thumb pressed against his palm . . ."

" Well ? "

Stanley laughed again.

" Why, the ball of my thumb, the ball only, was doctored with a little dab of crimson paint, kept fresh and damp with a drop of turps ! "

7. Write a précis of the following :

Through all time, if we read aright, sin was, is, will be, the parent of misery. This land of France calls itself

most Christian, and has crosses and cathedrals; but its
High-priest is some Roche-Aymon, some Necklace-Cardinal
Louis de Rohan. The voice of the poor, through long
years, ascends inarticulate, in *Jacqueries,* meal-mobs; low-
whimpering of infinite moan : unheeded of the Earth; not
unheeded of Heaven. Always moreover where the Millions
are wretched, there are the Thousands straitened, unhappy;
only the Units can flourish; or say rather, be ruined the
last. Industry, all noosed and haltered, as if it too were
some beast of chase for the mighty hunters of this world
to bait, and cut slices from,—cries passionately to these its
well paid guides and watchers, not, *Guide me ;* but, *Laissez
faire,* Leave me alone of *your* guidance ! What market
has Industry in this France ? For two things there may
be market and demand : for the coarser kind of field-
fruits, since the Millions will live : for the finer kinds of
luxury and spicery,—of multiform taste, from opera-
melodies down to racers and courtesans; since the Units
will be amused. It is at bottom but a mad state of
things. . . .

Remark, as acknowledged grounds of Hope, at bottom
mere precursors of Despair, this perpetual theorizing about
Man, the Mind of Man, Philosophy of Government, Progress of the Species, and such like; the main thinking
furniture of every head. . . . And now has not Jean
Jacques promulgated his new Evangel of a *Contrat Social ;*
explaining the whole mystery of Government, and how it
is *contracted* and bargained for—to universal satisfaction ?
Theories of Government ! Such have been, and will be;
in ages of decadence. Acknowledge them in their degree;
as processes of Nature, who does nothing in vain; as steps
in her great process. Meanwhile, what theory is so certain
as this, That all theories, were they never so earnest,
painfully elaborated, are, and, by the very conditions of
them, must be incomplete, questionable, and even false ?
Thou shalt know that this Universe is, what it professes
to be, an *infinite* one. Attempt not to swallow *it,* for thy
logical digestion; be thankful, if skilfully planting down
this and the other fixed pillar in the chaos, thou prevent
its swallowing *thee.* That a new young generation has
exchanged the Sceptic Creed, *What shall I believe ?* for

passionate Faith in this Gospel according to Jean Jacques, is a further step in the business; and betokens much.

Blessed also is Hope; and always from the beginning there was some Millennium prophesied; Millennium of Holiness; but (what is notable) never till this new Era, any Millennium of mere Ease and plentiful Supply. In such prophesied Lubberland of Happiness, Benevolence, and Vice cured of its deformity, trust not, my friends! Man is not what one calls a happy animal; his appetite for sweet victual is so enormous. How, in this wild Universe, which storms in on him, infinite, vague-menacing, shall poor man find, say not happiness, but existence, and footing to stand on, if it be not by girding himself together for continual endeavour and endurance? Woe, if in his heart there dwelt no devout Faith; if the word Duty had lost its meaning for him! For as to this of Sentimentalism, so useful for weeping with over romances and on pathetic occasions, it otherwise verily will avail nothing; nay less. The healthy heart that said to itself, "How healthy am I!" was already fallen into the fatallest sort of disease. Is not Sentimentalism twin-sister to Cant, if not one and the same with it : Cant, from which all falsehoods, imbecilities, abominations body themselves; from which no true thing *can* come? For Cant is itself properly a double-distilled Lie; the second-power of a Lie.

And now if a whole Nation fall into that? In such case, I answer, infallibly they will return out of it! For life is no cunningly-devised deception or self-deception : it is a great truth that thou art alive, that thou hast desires, necessities; neither can these subsist and satisfy themselves on delusions, but on fact. To fact, depend on it, we shall come back : to such fact, blessed or cursed, as we have wisdom for. The lowest, least blessed fact one knows of, on which necessitous mortals have ever based themselves, seems to be the primitive one of Cannibalism : That *I* can devour *Thee*. What if such Primitive Fact were precisely the one we had (with our improved methods) to revert to, and begin anew from !—THOMAS CARLYLE, *French Revolution.*

8. Write a précis of the following :

1. The parish council for a rural parish shall be elected from among the parochial electors of that parish or persons who have during the whole of the twelve months preceding the election resided in the parish, or within three miles thereof, and shall consist of a chairman and councillors, and the number of councillors shall be such as may be fixed from time to time by the county council, not being less than five nor more than fifteen.

2. No person shall be disqualified by sex or marriage for being elected or being a member of a parish council.

3. The term of office of a parish councillor shall be one year.

4. On the fifteenth day of April in each year (in this Act referred to as the ordinary day of coming into office of councillors) the parish councillors shall go out of office, and their places shall be filled by the newly elected councillors.

5. The parish councillors shall be elected by the parochial electors of the parish.

6. The election of parish councillors shall, subject to the provisions of this Act, be conducted according to rules framed under this Act for that purpose by the Local Government Board.

7. The parish council shall in every year, on or within seven days after the ordinary day of coming into office of councillors, hold an annual meeting.

8. At the annual meeting, the parish council shall elect, from their own body or from other persons qualified to be councillors of the parish, a chairman, who shall, unless he resigns, or ceases to be qualified, or becomes disqualified, continue in office until his successor is elected.

9. Every parish council shall be a body corporate by the name of the parish council, with the addition of the name of the parish, or if there is any doubt as to the latter name, of such name as the county council after consultation with the parish meeting of the parish direct, and shall have perpetual succession, and may hold and for the purposes of their powers and duties without licence in mortmain ; and any act of the council may be signified by an instrument executed at a meeting of the council, and under the

M

hands or, if an instrument under seal is required, under the hands and seals, of the chairman presiding at the meeting and two other members of the council.

9. Make a précis of the following report from *The Times* newspaper :

The Ordinary General Meeting of Selfridge Provincial Stores, Limited, was held yesterday in the Palm Court, Selfridge's, 400, Oxford Street, London, W.

Mr. H. Gordon Selfridge, the chairman, presided.

The Secretary (Mr. A. H. Youngman) having read the notice convening the meeting and the report of the auditors,

Mr. H. G. Selfridge, Jun. (managing director), said : Ladies and gentlemen,—With your consent I will take the annual report of our company that covers the 12 months that ended on August 31 last, as read.   (Agreed.)

The Selfridge Provincial Stores, Limited, is a holding company, owning 99·9 per cent. of the Ordinary share capital of 17 stores and shops in the London suburbs and the provinces—plus a proportion of their Preference capital. It engages in no trading on its own behalf; its activities are exercised through the management and direction of its subsidiaries. Its income is derived—with the exception of a small amount in connection with transfer fees—wholly from the dividends it receives from its shares in the companies it controls.   We have always included in our report an amalgamated account of the balance-sheets of our subsidiaries. It is printed just below the balance-sheet and profit and loss account of the Selfridge Provincial Stores, Limited, in the report that you have had in your possession now for some days.

The Net Profit

The total net profit of the businesses we control during the 12 months under review was £215,712 4s. This amount includes a sum of £18,605 that was made on the sale of a part of the property occupied at Streatham by Pratts. The sale was made at a figure that was in excess by that amount of what it had appeared in that business's books. Part of that profit has been reinvested in an improvement to the remainder; and the whole transaction has reflected itself in improved business and earnings. But this will be discussed a little later. For the moment I may say that this special item of £18,605 has properly entered into the profits of our branches.

INCREASED NUMBER AND LOWER VALUE OF INDIVIDUAL PURCHASES

The total of £215,712 is about £33,000 below a year ago —about 13 per cent. In view of the many things that have during the past 12 months tended to reduce the profitableness of business enterprise, your directors feel that this result is not one that calls for apology or regrets. Prices of commodities during the period under review have been falling and the purchasing power of the consumer is less than it has been since our company was formed. While the total sales in money of our branches are a little below what they were the year before, the amount of merchandise sold is greater than before, and the number of transactions has been much more than maintained. Last month, in the aggregate, we made nearly 50,000 transactions more than in the equivalent days in August of the year before. Last Saturday we made nearly 3,000 more than on the same Saturday of last year. And while the number of customers who are entering our branches and making purchases is so much more than maintaining itself in this way, it must be that our businesses are developing their popularity and each becoming more and more an institution in their various centres, and therefore developing their ability to make the most of the recovery that is bound to take place.

The trouble, of course, is that while the number of transactions is increasing, the value of each has decreased rather more. There are certain expenses which remain nearly constant, and others which increase in proportion with total volume. I may put it shortly and accurately by saying that the net profits of our branches have fallen, because the total amount of gross profit obtainable in the aggregate from their business has declined more than it has been possible for us to reduce the expenses.

One way in which it would have been possible for us to bring about a greater reduction of the expenses and which we have purposefully not undertaken has been in a general scheme of reduction of rates of salary or wage or general reduction of staff.

AVAILABLE BALANCE AND DIVIDEND

After paying, in the form of Preference dividends and Debenture interest to shareholders other than our company, £32,966, there is left available to us £182,745 7s. 8d.

Of this total we have left the substantial sum of nearly £44,000 in the books of our branches, and have used that sum in further depreciation, etc. And we have actually taken £138,831. This, plus about £400 in transfer fees makes our income £139,234 3s.

REDUCTION IN EXPENSES

The expenses of the Selfridge Provincial Stores, Limited, amount to £40,808. This is less by £14,000 than a year ago. Details of that expenditure are given on the profit and loss account, which is adjoined to the balance-sheet. If you turn to that you will see that interest on loans, etc., is £5,860. It was just over £15,000 last year; and this reduction is directly due to the conservative policy of not declaring away in dividends all our profits, but retaining in the business an important proportion. The item of income-tax is £28,139. It was £33,413 last year.

This reduction in the expenses of the holding company has resulted in our net income being £98,425 15s. 11d., which is about £1,700 more than last year.

Your directors are recommending that a dividend of 2½ per cent. be paid on the Ordinary shares of the company, and your directors have appropriated £50,000 for finally writing off the balance of the preliminary expenses. The disappearance of this item marks the attaining of one of our aims for the past six years. In the six years since the formation of our company in the autumn of 19.., we will have paid out dividends to our shareholders of £947,000, and we have as well written off entirely over £238,000 of preliminary expenses.

To wipe out these preliminary expenses has required using some of our carry-forward, which has been reduced from £9,387 to £1,563. But we think shareholders will be nearly as delighted as, quite frankly, we are that this item can no longer appear on our balance-sheet.

10. Make a précis of the following report from *The Times* newspaper :

The Nineteenth Ordinary General Meeting of the City of San Paulo Improvements and Freehold Land Company, Limited, was held yesterday at River Plate House, London, E.C.

Mr. Herbert Guedalla, F.C.A. (the chairman), said that owing to sales cancelled they had an actual increase in the book value of their freehold land of £12,594, so that the land now stood in the balance-sheet at a book value of £2,151,928. Although sales had been small during the year, the selling price showed a considerable appreciation in currency over the valuation.

All their land was within the confines of the City of San Paulo, and what they termed their unsold developed saleable area consisted of 930 acres spread over nine estates, some of which, owing to their situation and development, were bound to command high values. They also possessed a considerable area, amounting to 680 acres, of undeveloped land, which was taken at a nominal value, and which, in time to come, would undoubtedly prove an important asset. In his opinion a new valuation at the present time would show a material increase over that made for the previous year, but he was bound to add that an analysis of the situation showed that, so far, the value of freehold land in San Paulo had not responded to the fall in currency exchange. That was due to two factors, the first and foremost being that Brazil was fortunate in that she was practically a self-supporting country, and the cost of living had hardly altered at all despite the fall of 50 per cent. in monetary exchange values. Secondly, Brazilian companies or individuals owning land, with their capital in milreis, had, for various reasons, chiefly monetary, been offering land on attractive terms, and that had undoubtedly tended to keep down prices.

SALES CONDITIONS AND PROSPECTS

While trade conditions continued to be very poor, people with money preferred to keep their cash with the banks owing to the uncertainties of the situation. In other countries where exchange had fallen the value of land had adjusted itself accordingly over a certain period. Circumstances in Brazil were somewhat different, but he could not help thinking that in time the value of the company's land would attain a value more nearly in relation to the value of the currency. Therefore the company were continuing their policy of not hastening the sale of their developed properties, but where, of course, some desirable client, particularly one who wished to build, came forward with an offer they were inclined to accept it because such a sale helped to maintain the value of their properties.

With regard to the question of exchange, it was most difficult to prophesy as to the future. The directors found it impossible at present to form any reliable estimate as to what amount should be allocated out of reserve to deal with that matter. Their main asset was their freehold land, and in currency at 6d. it was worth much more than the amount at which it stood in the balance-sheet. Their other big asset consisted of debtors for land and houses sold and house-construction loans. Those were secured debts, payable with interest by monthly instalments over six or seven years. It was their opinion that in due course the value of freehold land would adjust itself according to the exchange position. That applied also to the improvements and to the houses which they owned.

THE FUTURE OF BRAZIL

If they could forecast with any accuracy what the fluctuations in exchange might be in the next six or seven years during the collection of their debts, the company would be in a very fortunate position, but it must suffice at the present moment to know that in their opinion their reserves were more than ample to meet any contingency in that respect. Recent circumstances—he might almost say daily circumstances—had rendered it much more difficult to estimate the question of the relative value of the milreis to the sterling of this country.

The year under review, and the current year to date, had been a period of great uncertainty, but he did think, without being too optimistic, that Brazil, with her vast natural resources which were being exploited in several new directions, would emerge at no distant date from the depression which now existed. Therefore he looked forward to a restoration of confidence and to the resumption of the operations of the company on a normal scale.

The report was unanimously adopted.

CHAPTER X

PRÉCIS WRITING (*continued*)

Précis of Correspondence. In a number of examinations it was usual to give a series of letters from which a précis was to be made. This form of exercise, however, seems to have lost favour with examiners, but as it may possibly arise in the future, it is desirable for students to be prepared for it.

The main rule to be followed is that the précis must be drawn up in the form of a smooth connected narrative, and not letter by letter. It is usually possible to extract one key letter from the series, and to make this the basis of the whole précis. It is probably on account of this fact, which makes the exercise particularly easy, that it has almost disappeared from present-day examination papers.

A perusal of the following example will show clearly exactly what is required in this form of exercise.

Make a précis of the following correspondence :

From John Hammond, Solicitor, London.
To the Secretary, Arthur Underwood & Co., Ltd.

24th April, 19 . .

re The Commercial Corporation, Ltd.

Can you not let me have a cheque for the *balance of my Sydney Agents' charges* as they are pressing me for a settlement ?

From Arthur Underwood & Co., Ltd.
To John Hammond.

28th April, 19 . .

re The Commercial Corporation, Ltd.

Replying to your letter of the 24th instant, we beg to remind you that *we are waiting for particulars* of the account rendered by Messrs. Robinson & Co., your Sydney Agents.

Our Auditors comment as follows on our Balance Sheet for last year :—

" Litigation in Australia.

" With reference to this figure in your accounts, we are " strongly of opinion that Messrs. Robinson & Company " should be asked to furnish you with further details of " the items for costs contained in their Accounts."

The item to which the auditors particularly refer we think is the one in the statement dated 6th February, 19 . .

" 19 . . May⎫
   to   ⎬ To costs herein . . . £1,555."
" 19 . . Dec.⎭

Will you kindly ask your agents about this, and also *how the £1,600 paid into the Equity Court was disposed of.* There is, we believe, £500 or £550 remaining to our credit. We suppose the balance was applied towards payment of the Opponents' costs in the first action.

From John Hammond, Solicitor.
To the Secretary,
Messrs. Arthur Underwood & Co., Ltd., London.

30th April, 19 . .

re The Commercial Corporation, Ltd.

Referring to my interview with you on the 17th March, I shall be glad to hear whether you wish any, and if so, what further information with regard to the *balance of costs* due to me, namely, *£221* in connection with the proceedings conducted by my Agents in Sydney on my behalf against the above named Corporation.

It is more than a year since the matter was concluded and I am anxious to have it settled up.

Kindly let me hear from you.

From Arthur Underwood & Co., Ltd.
To John Hammond.

10th May, 19 . .

Replying to your letter of the 30th April, I now beg to hand you a copy of a letter dated 6th May, from Messrs. Francis & Co., the Company's Auditors, in further reference to the bill of costs in the action against the Commercial Corporation, Ltd.

I shall be glad if you will ask your agents to *furnish details of their account* including the item of £*1,555*, and *Counsel's fees £1,770.*

Will you please also *render an account* in respect of the sums of £*25*, £*60 and £50* paid you on March 21st, 19 . ., December 7th, 19 . ., and July 6th, 19 . . respectively.

From Messrs. Francis & Co., Chartered Accountants.
To the Secretary, Arthur Underwood & Co., Ltd.

London, 6th May, 19 . .

In reply to your letter of May 1st, with its enclosures, we note Messrs. Robinson & Company's remarks in answer to your enquiry as to how the item of costs amounting to £1,555 is arrived at, and as to how the £1,600 paid into the Equity Court was disposed of. The correspondence and statements which you have shown us appear to dispose satisfactorily of the latter sum of £1,600 but we are still of opinion that Messrs. Robinson & Co. should be asked to furnish details of their account, including *the item of £1,555* which is simply stated as being "for costs" without any detail. We cannot see any reason why these particulars should not be supplied to you, as they must of course be available to Messrs. Robinson & Company.

There are other items in the latest statement of account which you have received from them which appear to require detailing as, for example, the large sum paid for Counsel's fees. We also understand from you that you have raised several queries on their accounts, some of which have not been settled. It would seem desirable that when applying to Messrs. Robinson & Co. for the details above referred to, you should also obtain complete answers to any outstanding queries.

From John Hammond, Solicitor.
To the Secretary, Arthur Underwood & Co., Ltd.

12th May, 19 . .

re The Commercial Corporation, Ltd.

I am in receipt of your letter of the 10th instant enclosing copy of a letter from the Company's Auditors in reference to my Agents' Costs in the action against The Commercial Corporation, Ltd.

By this week's mail I am writing to my *Agents requesting them to furnish me* with the details you ask for.

With regard to the amounts paid to me they have been absorbed by my costs and disbursements, and I shall be glad if you will advise me whether you require an account showing this or whether you require a detailed bill.

From Arthur Underwood & Co., Ltd.
To John Hammond, London.

13th May, 19 . .

re The Commercial Corporation, Ltd.

In reference to your letter of the 12th instant, we shall be glad to have a *detailed bill of your costs and disbursements.*

From John Hammond, London.
To the Secretary, Arthur Underwood & Co., Ltd.

18th May, 19 . .

In answer to your letter of the 13th instant, I enclose herewith, as requested, my *detailed bill of costs.*

From John Hammond, Solicitor.
To the Secretary, Arthur Underwood & Co., Ltd.

17th February, 19 . .

re The Commercial Corporation, Ltd.

Owing to the death of their Accountant, my Agents have *not been able* hitherto *to supply the details* asked for by your Auditors, but I have now received them and shall be glad to hear *if I should post them to you.*

As the amount due to my Agents has been debited by them against me, it is of the utmost importance to me to have their account settled and paid to me as quickly as possible.

From Arthur Underwood & Co., Ltd.
To John Hammond, Esq., London.

27th February, 19 . .

re The Commercial Corporation, Ltd.

Replying to your letter of the 17th instant, *we do not admit that any sum is due* to you or your agents in respect of the action brought by us against The Commercial Corporation, Ltd., in the year 19 . .

From John Hammond.
To the Secretary, Arthur Underwood & Co., Ltd.

28th February, 19 . .

I am quite at a loss to understand your letter. If you will refer to your letters of 28th April, 19 . ., 10th and 13th May, 19 . ., and my various letters to you, you will see that your Company is perfectly well aware of its indebtedness to me and my Agents.

In accordance with the request contained in yours of the 10th May, *I now forward* you by registered post under separate cover, *the details asked for* by you up to October, 19 . ., £3,959, also payment to Smithers £839 and to the Equity Court £1,600.

You will see from the enclosed account rendered me that my Agents have debited my account with *£921,* as

against which *I have received* from you *£500 and £200*
leaving *£221* due (see my letter of 30th April, 19 . .).

Apart from this, you asked me on the 13th May, 19 . .,
for a detailed bill of my own costs, and this was sent you on
18th May, 19 . ., but no settlement was ever made, though
promised by you more than once.   This was only a small
amount.

In view of your repudiation of the balance due to me, I
regret to say *I shall insist on a prompt settlement*, and
failing this, I must have recourse to proceedings.

From the Chairman, Arthur Underwood & Co., Ltd.
To John Hammond.

March 1st, 19 . .

Referring to our interview yesterday, I now enclose, as
arranged, my *Company's cheque for £100 in full settlement*
of all outstanding claims against this Company in respect of
the action brought by us against the Commercial Corporation
Ltd., in Australia.

From John Hammond.
To the Chairman, Arthur Underwood & Co., Ltd.

March 2nd, 19 . .

I thank you for your favour of the 1st instant enclosing
cheque value £100 in full discharge of Messrs. Robinson &
Company's and my own accounts in the matter of the
Commercial Corporation, Ltd.

Précis

Costs in re The Commercial Corporation, Ltd.

In April 19 . . John Hammond, Solicitor, London,
requested Arthur Underwood Ltd. to remit the balance
of his Sydney Agent's charges amounting to £221.
Before doing this Underwood's required further details,
particularly as to costs of £1,555, Counsel's fees £1,770,
how the sum of £1,600 paid in to the Equity Court was
disposed of and of the £135 paid to Hammond in three
different amounts

In May 19 . . Hammond supplied his own bill of costs. About nine months later he received his agent's details, the delay being due to the death of their accountant, and suggested posting them to Underwood's. They, however, denied all liability, whereupon Hammond pointed out how the £221 arose, and also referred to his own unsettled costs, threatening proceedings for recovery of the amount due. In March 19 . ., as the result of an interview with the chairman of Underwood's, Hammond accepted £100 in full settlement of both his and his agent's charges.

It should be noted how the essence of the correspondence has been extracted, and how unimportant and irrelevant matter has been discarded.

Summaries, Telegrams, etc. These must be distinguished from précis, in that whereas a précis must be written in good English, a summary or telegram may be ruthlessly condensed by the omission of words and phrases. The main point is to ensure that the summary is understandable, and that nothing of vital importance is omitted. It may be mentioned that, in some examinations, a summary is asked for when what is needed is a précis. It is, however, usually quite a simple thing to determine what is wanted by the examiner, since, where a fairly lengthy passage is given, it obviously calls for a précis, whereas a short passage such as the following must be summarised.

Example. Reduce the following as near as possible to twelve words :

Your most welcome cable duly received last night fortunately before left office. All of us strongly united opinion should close with admittedly generous Walbrook offer. Would help Walbrook firm turn corner lean time and recognition helping hand make valuable connection both ways them and us. Cable steps taken complete final settlement.

" Closing with Walbrook would help both sides. Cable steps taken to complete."

The cable has been reduced to twelve words as required. Any further omission might puzzle the recipient.

QUESTIONS

1. Make a précis of the following correspondence :—

I.   From H. Bell (Agent), to Secretary, Charlton Mines, Ltd.

18th October, 19 . .

T. SMITH'S ESTATE

I visited the mine on the 10th inst., and have to point out that since my previous visit six months ago no practical effort has been made to do anything in reference to the restoration of the surface of the land, and I now notice that when the mechanical digger is working, no attempt whatever is being made to preserve the turf and soil. It is all being dug up promiscuously by the digger, and conveyed over into heaps on the other side. I must point out that this is a deliberate breach of the covenant set out in clause 5 of the lease between Mr. Smith and yourselves, which reads, " And whenever any land shall cease to be used for the purpose of this demise, the lessee shall restore the surface thereof to its original state as far as practicable and with all reasonable despatch." I have discussed the matter with Mr. Smith, and it is quite impossible that he could allow the whole of the land over which you pass to be rendered derelict. I shall be in Sheffield next week, and propose to call and discuss this matter with you.

II.   From the Secretary, Charlton Mines, Ltd., to H. Bell.

19th October, 19 . .

I am in receipt of yours of yesterday, and shall be glad if you can arrange to meet the Chairman and myself at this office on Wednesday next, 24th inst., in order to discuss fully the question of the restoration of the surface of Mr. Smith's land.

III. From the Secretary, Charlton Mines, Ltd., to H. Bell.

27th October, 19 . .

T. SMITH'S ESTATE

Referring to our conversation on Wednesday last, I am instructed to offer you the following terms in lieu of the restoration of the surface of the land.

1. We to pay the sum of £20 per acre for all land unrestored at the present time, and for any land worked by us in the future, it being incumbent on us to declare, when we finish mining each acre, whether we intend to restore it or not.

2. In the event of our deciding not to restore, you to have the choice of equivalent acres from adjoining lands, not on the main road, which are the freehold property of this company, the unrestored land becoming the property of this company. An alternative proposal for future working might be based on an increased royalty payable to you of, say, $\frac{1}{2}d.$ per ton in lieu of restoration. I shall be glad if you will place these proposals before Mr. Smith, and let me know his views as soon as possible.

IV. From H. Bell, to the Secretary, Charlton Mines, Ltd.

28th November, 19 . .

I visited the mine yesterday in company with Mr. Smith, and discussed with him the question of payment for the land in lieu of restoration, as dealt with in your letter of the 27th ult. Any of the proposals set out would mean a variation of the lease, and the matter will therefore be referred to Mr. Smith's solicitors, from whom you will hear in due course.

V. From the Secretary, Charlton Mines, Ltd., to H. Lawton & Co., Solicitors.

15th January, 19 . .

T. SMITH'S ESTATE

On the 27th October last we submitted certain proposals to Mr. Bell regarding the restoration of the surface of Mr. Smith's land. We understand you are dealing with this matter, and shall be glad to have Mr. Smith's views on the proposals.

VI.   From H. Lawton & Co., Solicitors, to the Secretary, Charlton Mines, Ltd.

17*th January,* 19 . .

T. SMITH'S ESTATE

In reply to yours of the 15th inst., Mr. Bell is on active service, and with Mr. Smith's concurrence the matter is being left over until his return.   Everyone is so busy just now, and the labour shortage so acute that we feel sure you will concur in this decision.

VII.   From H. Bell, to the Secretary, Charlton Mines, Ltd.

20*th February,* 19 . .

T. SMITH'S ESTATE

Mr. Smith is of the opinion that the question of restoration must now be settled, and after careful consideration of the terms set out in your letter of 27th Oct., 19 . ., I am not disposed to recommend Mr. Smith's acceptance of any of them.   I will take the opportunity of calling at your office on the 26th inst., at 2 p.m., when I shall be in Sheffield, and I shall be glad if your Chairman can meet me there.

VIII.   From the Secretary, Charlton Mines, Ltd., to H. Bell.

10*th March,* 19 . .

With reference to your interview with my Chairman on the 26th ult., and your suggestion that Mr. Smith would be prepared to accept the surface rights on certain of this company's freehold land in lieu of restoration, I am instructed to submit the following for your consideration. The land which needs restoring under the terms of our lease is situated well back from the main road, and your suggestion that field No. 62 would be suitable for exchange is inequitable in the ratio of acre for acre; but we are prepared to consider your proposal on the basis of two acres of the unrestored land for one acre of our freehold land situate on the main road.   Please let me hear from you on this point.

IX.   From H. Bell, to the Secretary, Charlton Mines, Ltd

15*th March,* 19 . .

I have yours of the 10th inst.   I do not agree that the exchange as suggested is inequitable, but in view of the fact that the fields on either side of field No. 62 belong to Mr.

N

Smith, and as he is anxious to acquire this field, he is prepared to accept your offer. I will write you shortly regarding the remaining 27·642 acres of unrestored land, with regard to which Mr. Smith is not prepared to consider any exchange.

X. From H. Bell, to the Secretary, Charlton Mines, Ltd.
2nd May, 19 . .

With reference to the question of the covenant in Mr. Smith's lease for restoration of the surface, I have considered the matter with Mr. Smith and his Solicitors, and have instructions to write you thereon. By the terms of the lease the Lessees are bound to restore the surface where they have worked. I am sending you a schedule and plan showing the area worked and in occupation by your company, and not restored in accordance with the covenant in the lease. The area amounts to 27·642 acres, excluding the ten acres we are surrendering to you in exchange for field No. 62. The offer I make on Mr. Smith's behalf without prejudice, in regard to the 27·642 acres, is as follows :—

1. That in lieu of restoration of the area shown on the plan in accordance with the covenant of the lease, a sum of £35 per acre shall be paid to Mr. Smith, and that this area shall be fenced off from the rest of the Lessor's land and planted with young trees at the cost of the Lessees.
2. With regard to future operations under the lease, all land, except such as is in the actual occupation and use of the Lessees for mining purposes, shall from time to time be restored, in accordance with the covenant of the lease, with all reasonable despatch.

XI. From the Secretary, Charlton Mines, Ltd., to H. Bell.
10th May, 19 . .

T. SMITH'S LEASE

I am in receipt of yours of the 2nd inst., with enclosure. We are not disposed to consider the terms put forward unless they can be applied to the whole of the land to be worked in the future as well as that already worked. You must be quite cognisant of the fact of the impossibility, except at an enormous cost, of restoring any land that has been worked by a mechanical digger, and we wish to have this question finally settled. I append a schedule showing five companies, who worked under almost identical conditions, together with the payment per acre made by them in lieu of restoration. You will note that in no case has this exceeded £25.

Name of Company.	Amount per acre paid in lieu of restoration.
Illington Quarries, Ltd. . .	£25
Torrington Mines, Ltd. . . .	£22
Firmley Ironstone Co., Ltd. . .	£18
Mirton Mines, Ltd. . . .	£20
Fulchester Quarries, Ltd. . .	£24

XII. From H. Lawton & Co., Solicitors, to Secretary, Charlton Mines, Ltd.

10*th September*, 19 . .

T. SMITH'S LEASE

We are instructed by Mr. T. Smith to offer you the following terms in connection with the breach of covenant in the lease :—

1. That in lieu of restoring the land which has been worked to the present date in accordance with the covenant in the lease, the Company shall pay to the Lessor the sum of £35 per acre, and shall fence and plant the land with young trees.

2. That the Lessor is willing that the Company shall, if it so desires, continue to work his land on similar terms in lieu of restoration, the Lessor retaining the right to call upon the Company to revert to the conditions of the lease at any time, by giving six months' notice in writing.

3. That the Company shall pay the charges of Mr. Bell and ourselves incurred in this matter.

XIII. From the Secretary, Charlton Mines, Ltd., to H. Lawton & Co.

12*th September*, 19 . .

T. SMITH'S ESTATE

I am in receipt of yours of yesterday, and am instructed to inform you that the Board of this Company accepts the terms offered therein.   The draft deed, releasing us from our liability under the original lease, should be forwarded when ready to our Solicitors, Messrs. Tomkins & Brown, 12, Cutler Street, Sheffield.

XIV.   From the Secretary, Charlton Mines, Ltd., to Tomkins & Brown.

22nd September, 19 . .

T. SMITH'S ESTATE

I note in the draft deed forwarded by you that we are required to level the ground before planting the trees.   This has never been mentioned in the discussions which have taken place, and we are not prepared to undertake this. With this clause deleted, we are prepared to agree to the draft.

XV.   From the Secretary, Charlton Mines, Ltd., to Tomkins & Brown.

29th September, 19 . .

We note that Messrs. Lawton & Co. have agreed to delete the clause as to our levelling the ground before planting. We will complete the Lessor's copy of the deed immediately on receipt.

2. Make a summary of the following, reducing it as nearly as possible to twelve words :—" Thank you for your kind invitation.   I shall be happy to accept it, and will accordingly leave here at 10.50 and arrive at your place at 12.30.   I will certainly do as you wish and bring the picture in question with me."

3. Distinguish between a summary, a précis and a telegram.

4. Write a series of about six letters showing negotiations for the sale of a house.   The letters should show respectively a request from a prospective buyer; the agent's reply with price; a counter offer of a lower price; a further offer by the agent at a price somewhere between that originally asked and that offered; acceptance of this offer.

5. Make a précis of the letters written in answer 4.

SECTION III

MISCELLANEOUS

CHAPTER XI

PARAPHRASING

A PARAPHRASE is an interpretation of the thoughts and feelings of a passage, usually of poetry, in simple prose. It is an exercise both in the writing of English and in the sympathetic understanding of another writer's thoughts. It is thus an aid to the mastery of style and composition, and also to the appreciation of good literature. To write a good paraphrase we need a clear understanding of the original, and a command of English which will enable us to produce a carefully worded and proportioned composition that will not be a mere mutilation of beautiful literature.

A paraphrase is not just a word-for-word translation. The mere substitution of one word for another which is more or less synonymous is useless, and ruins rather than explains the passage. It must be treated, not word by word or even sentence by sentence, but as a homogeneous whole.

The chief aim is to get at the essential point of the passage, *i.e.* the underlying train of thought that gives it unity. Try to put yourself in the writer's place; ask yourself: " What is the writer trying to say ? What mood is he trying to express ? " When you have answered these questions, then will be the time to turn to details of phraseology.

Notes. 1. Do not attempt to write a word until you have a thorough understanding of the meaning and

191

spirit of the passage. Read it carefully several times, until you have acquired this.

2. Note the main stages in the development of the thought. Draw up mentally, or better still on paper, a skeleton outline of this. When this central thread of ideas has been grasped, difficult details will fall more easily into place.

3. Now turn your attention to details, until you see clearly the significance of every word and figure of speech.

4. The actual writing can now be commenced. The finished paraphrase must explain clearly and fully the development of the thought. It must be free from figurative language—*all* metaphors, etc., must be turned into plain prose. Remember that apostrophe is a figure of speech—it is best to turn such an expression into indirect speech, or to omit it by means of some more impersonal construction. Above all, the paraphrase must be a well-written, well-arranged whole, with the argument presented in logical order—occasionally some re-arrangement of the original may be necessary for this —and prominence given to the important points.

5. Try to reproduce something of the atmosphere of the original. Choose your words and model your style so that they are in harmony with the tone of the original —a serious style for a serious passage, a light style for light verse, and so on.

6. *Length.* This depends on the degree of conciseness of the original. Often the language of poetry is so condensed, by the use of metaphor and concise construction not permissible in prose, that a prose rendering will occupy considerably more space than the original. On the other hand, poetry often employs, for the sake of decorative effect, a wealth of imagery that in prose would be tedious and unnecessary.

Two Types of Paraphrase. The distinction between the close paraphrase and free interpretation of a passage should be appreciated. The latter is probably the more commonly required in modern examination papers; in such cases the examinee is usually informed that a close paraphrase is not required. The procedure is basically the same in both. We need to understand equally the general import of the whole and the point of every detail. The difference lies merely in the degree of closeness with which the original passage is followed. In a close paraphrase the original order and the various details are followed fairly faithfully, but *not* so as to reproduce a mere word-for-word translation. The free rendering, however, demands merely the statement of the substance as clearly and effectively as possible without necessarily adhering to the original order, or interpreting details of imagery, etc. In a close paraphrase a close rendering is wanted, whereas much more latitude is allowed and exerted in a free interpretation. Remember not to attempt a close paraphrase unless this is specifically asked for.

In the following examples we give first a close paraphrase, and then a free rendering of the same passage. The former represents the extreme degree of fidelity with which the original should be treated.

Examples :

1. A fairly short, simple example :

We live in deeds, not words; in thoughts, not breaths;
In feelings, not in figures on a dial.
We should count time by heart-throbs. He most lives
Who thinks most, feels the noblest, acts the best.
When imperfection ceaseth, heaven begins.

First let us find the essential thought. After reading the passage we find that the writer is saying that the excellence of life depends on how we use it rather than on its duration.

PARAPHRASE

Deeds, thoughts, and feelings, not mere talking, breathing, or living to a great age, are the essentials of life. The length of life should be measured by its intensity, for his life is the fullest whose thoughts, feelings and actions are the finest. The achievement of perfect life means the beginning of heaven.

The thought may be rendered more freely:

If we would measure our span of life we should take into account not its mere duration, but what we have made of it—the nobility and intensity of our thoughts, feelings and deeds. By attaining perfection in these, we live to the full, but not only this; we reach heaven, which is really just life free from imperfection.

2. The world's a bubble and the life of Man
      Less than a span:
   In his conception wretched, from the womb
      So to the tomb;
   Curst from his cradle, and brought up to years,
      With cares and fears.
   Who then to frail mortality shall trust,
      But limns on water, or but writes in dust.
   Yet whilst with sorrow here we live opprest,
      What life is best?
   Courts are but only superficial schools,
      To dandle fools;
   The rural parts are turned into a den
      Of savage men;

And where's a city from foul vice so free,
 But may be termed the worst of all the three?
Domestic cares afflict the husband's bed,
 Or pains his head;
Those that live single take it for a curse,
 Or do things worse.
Some would have children; those that have them moan,
 Or wish them gone:
What is it then to have, or have no wife,
 But single thraldom, or a double strife?
But our affections still at home to please
 Is a disease:
To cross the seas to any foreign soil,
 Peril and toil:
Wars with their noise affright us; when they cease
 We are worse in peace:
What then remains but that we still should cry
 For being born, or being born, to die?

The first verse describes the transience, futility and wretchedness of life. The next stage is an analysis of the miseries associated with the various manners of life, leading to the conclusion that death is all we can look forward to.

CLOSE PARAPHRASE

The world and man are but transient; in addition, he is in misery from the beginning until the end of life. He is born under a curse; his years of childhood and youth are never free from anxiety. Thus, he who puts his faith in mortal things will be deceived, for his deeds will soon be forgotten.

Yet how can we best spend our time while we are afflicted with the misery of living? The glories of the court are but shallow amusement for fools. The country districts are all sunk in barbarism. Even worse are the cities, so infested with vice is every one.

The husband is afflicted with domestic and bodily troubles. The unmarried complain of their bad luck, or fall more deeply into sin. Those without children desire them; those that have them curse the fact and wish themselves childless. The single man gains from his condition merely the necessity of bearing his slavery alone; to the married, wedlock gives a life of strife.

We dislike having to take our pleasures at home; but to go abroad entails danger and discomfort. We are frightened by the tumult of war, yet we are worse off when it is over.

There is nothing to do but regret our birth, and, that being irremediable, to look forward to death.

Free Interpretation

Life is a futile, transient thing, and, like everything else in this world, soon passes into oblivion. Even while it lasts mortal life is spent in misery from birth to death. Thus worldly hopes can bring but transient success, soon utterly obliterated.

So wretched is it that, no matter what our station, there is nothing noble or pleasurable in living—our choice lies between the superficial glamour of the court, the viciousness of the city, and the barbarism of country life.

In domestic life, all men alike—married and unmarried, with children and without—complain of their wretched lot, and envy the better fortune of others. Not only is life full of discontent, but peril and hardship are never absent—at home and abroad, in war and in peace.

Such being our condition, we should curse the day on which we were born, for the only thing worth looking forward to is death.

Pitfalls. 1. Do not include ideas not stated or implied in the original.

2. Do not change a word merely for the sake of changing it, when the sense is not brought out more clearly. For instance, if the original passage contains the word " donkey," there would probably be no point in substituting the word " ass."

3. On the other hand, do not include entire phrases and sentences with next to no change in wording.

Some of the phrases employed where a free rendering is required are :—" Express in simple prose." " Tell the story of the following poem." " Express the thought conveyed in the following."

QUESTIONS

Unless otherwise required, a free prose rendering of each of the following should be given :

1. O, who can hold a fire in his hand
   By thinking on the frosty Caucasus ?
   Or cloy the hungry edge of appetite
   By bare imagination of a feast ?
   Or wallow naked in December snow
   By thinking on fantastic summer's heat ?
   O, no ! The apprehension of the good
   Owes but the greater feeling to the worse ;
   Fell sorrow's tooth doth never rankle more
   Than when it bites, but lanceth not the sore.

2. It's wiser being good than bad ;
      It's safer being meek than fierce :
   It's fitter being sane than mad.
      My own hope is a sun will pierce
   The thickest cloud earth ever stretched ;
      That, after Last, returns the First,
   Though a wide compass round be fetched ;
      That what began best, can't end worst,
   Nor what God blessed once, prove accursed.

3. This world a hunting is,
   The prey poor man, the Nimrod fierce is Death ;
   His speedy greyhounds are
   Lust, sickness, envy, care,
   Strife that ne'er falls amiss,
   With all those ills which haunt us while we breathe,
   Now if by chance we fly,
   Of these the eager chase,
   Old age with stealing pace
   Casts up his nets and there we panting die.

4. Dreams are but interludes which Fancy makes ;
   When monarch Reason sleeps, this mimic wakes :
   Compounds a medley of disjointed things,
   A mob of cobblers, and a court of kings :
   Light fumes are merry, grosser fumes are sad :
   Both are the reasonable soul run mad ;
   And many monstrous forms in sleep we see,
   That neither were, nor are, nor e'er can be.
   Sometimes forgotten things long cast behind
   Rush forward to the brain, and come to mind.
   The nurse's legends are for truths received,
   And the man dreams but what the boy believed.
   Sometimes we but rehearse a former play,
   The night restores our actions done by day ;
   As hounds in sleep will open for their prey.
   In short, the farce of dreams is of a piece,
   Chimeras all ; and more absurd, or less.

5.   I never may believe
   These antique fables, nor these fairy toys.
   Lovers and madmen have such seething brains,
   Such shaping fantasies, that apprehend
   More than cool reason ever comprehends.
   The lunatic, the lover and the poet,
   Are of imagination all compact :
   One sees more devils than vast Hell can hold,
   That is, the madman ; the lover, all as frantic,
   Sees Helen's beauty in a brow of Egypt :
   The poet's eye, in a fine frenzy rolling,

Doth glance from heaven to earth, from earth to heaven;
And, as imagination bodies forth
The forms of things unknown, the poet's pen
Turns them to shapes, and gives to airy nothing
A local habitation and a name.
Such tricks hath strong imagination,
That, if it would but apprehend some joy,
It comprehends some bringer of that joy;
Or in the night, imagining some fear,
How easy is a bush supposed a bear !

6. When I have fears that I may cease to be
    Before my pen has gleaned my teeming brain,
 Before high-piled books, in charact'ry,
    Hold like rich garners the full ripened grain;
 When I behold, upon the night's starred race,
    Huge cloudy symbols of a high romance,
 And think that I may never live to trace
    Their shadows, with the magic hand of chance;
 And when I feel, fair creature of an hour !
    That I shall never look upon thee more,
 Never have relish in the faery power
    Of unreflecting love !—then on the shore
 Of the wide world I stand alone, and think,
    Till Love and Fame to nothingness do sink.

7. It is not growing like a tree,
    In bulk, doth make men better be;
 Or standing long, an oak, three hundred year,
    To fall a log at last, dry, bald and sere;
        A lily of a day
        Is fairer far in May,
 Although it fall and die that night
 It was the plant and flower of light.
 In small proportions we just beauties see;
    And in short measures life may perfect be.

8. My heart leaps up when I behold
    A rainbow in the sky;
 So was it when my life began;
    So is it now I am a man;

So be it when I shall grow old,
    Or let me die !
The Child is Father of the Man ;
    And I could wish my days to be
Bound each to each by natural piety.

9. (a) Paraphrase the following, and (b) give the gist of it
in your own words :

Sweet stream, that winds through yonder glade,
Apt emblem of a virtuous maid—
Silent and chaste she steals along,
Far from the world's gay busy throng :
With gentle yet prevailing force,
Intent upon her destined course ;
Graceful and useful all she does,
Blessing and blest where'er she goes ;
Pure-bosom'd as that watery glass,
And Heaven reflected in her face.

10. She is not fair to outward view
    As many maidens be ;
Her loveliness I never knew
    Until she smiled on me.
O then I saw her eye was bright,
A well of love, a spring of light.

But now her looks are coy and cold,
    To mine they ne'er reply,
And yet I cease not to behold
    The love-light in her eye ;
Her very frowns are fairer far
Than smiles of other maidens are.

11. When he who adores thee has left but the name,
    Of his fault and his sorrows behind,
O ! say wilt thou weep, when they darken the fame
    Of a life that for thee was resign'd ?
Yes, weep, and however my foes may condemn,
    Thy tears shall efface their decree ;
For Heaven can witness, though guilty to them,
    I have been but too faithful to thee.

12. Now the last day of many days,
    All beautiful and bright as thou,
        The loveliest and the last, is dead,
    Rise, Memory, and write its praise !
    Up—to thy wonted work ! come, trace
        The epitaph of glory fled,
    For now the Earth has changed its face,
        A frown is on the Heaven's brow.

13. On a poet's lips I slept
    Dreaming like a love-adept
    In the sound his breathing kept ;
    Nor seeks nor finds he mortal blisses,
    But feeds on the aerial kisses
    Of shapes that haunt Thought's wildernesses.
    He will watch from dawn to gloom
    The lake-reflected sun illume
    The yellow bees in the ivy-bloom,
        Nor heed nor see what things they be—
    But from these create he can
    Forms more real than living Man,
        Nurslings of immortality !

14. Give me a golden pen, and let me lean
        On heap'd up flowers, in regions clear, and far ;
        Bring me a tablet whiter than a star,
    Or hand of hymning angel, when 'tis seen
    The silver strings of heavenly harp atween ;
        And let there glide by many a pearly car,
        Pink robes, and wavy hair, and diamond jar,
    And half-discovered wings, and glances keen.
    The while let music wander round my ears,
        And as it reaches each delicious ending,
        Let me write down a line of glorious tone,
    And full of many wonders of the spheres :
        For what a height my spirit is contending !
        'Tis not content so soon to be alone.

15. As travellers oft look back at eve,
        When eastward darkly going,
    To gaze upon that light they leave
        Still faint behind them glowing—
    o

So, when the close of pleasure's day
   To gloom hath near consign'd us,
We turn to catch one fading ray
   Of joy that's left behind us.

16. I can give not what men call love;
      But wilt thou accept not
   The worship the heart lifts above
      And the Heavens reject not—
   The desire of the moth for the star,
      Or the night for the morrow,
   The devotion to something afar,
      From the sphere of our sorrow?

17. Make a close paraphrase of Nos. 10, 12 and 14.

CHAPTER XII

WORDS

WORDS are the means by which we express ourselves in writing, and it is essential that we gain a sure command of them, and a clear understanding of their exact shades of meaning. The ability to select just the right words to express our meaning in a particular context is a very great aid in composition. Lack of this ability leads to clumsy expression and such errors as malapropism—the incorrect use of words not understood by the writer.

As if to emphasise the importance of a knowledge of words and their meanings, examiners often set questions in which candidates are required to give evidence of such knowledge, usually by distinguishing words easily confused, or by giving the meanings of uncommon words. The only sure method of attaining a command of words and a wide vocabulary is the free use of the dictionary. Whenever you meet a word the meaning of which is unfamiliar, note it, and learn its exact meaning. Take particular care to distinguish between words spelt similarly, and words almost synonymous; *e.g.*, *ingenious, ingenuous; illusion, delusion.*

Note also the *use* of words. Many words are so very nearly synonymous that the dictionary cannot clearly indicate the fine shades of difference. Often words which appear synonymous in the dictionary possess a very definite difference in usage. For instance, *spurious*

203

and *fictitious* could both be defined as *false*, but we speak of *spurious coins*, not *fictitious coins*, of *fictitious characters* in a novel, not *spurious characters*.

Remember that no two words mean exactly the same thing. Note the shades of difference in such groups as *find, discover, invent, create*. Often the difference is one of intensity, as " I *told* him to do it," " I *ordered* him to do it," " I *commanded* him to do it."

The following is a list of some of the words easily confused :

1. *Acquaintance, companion, friend.* Here the difference is one of intensity.

2. *Antiquated, obsolete. Antiquated* means something out of fashion, *e.g.* " He drove an antiquated car." *Obsolete*: something not now used, *e.g.* " That model is not now made ; it is obsolete."

3. *Complexity, complication.* Both convey the sense of intricacy, but *complication* rather suggests the idea of disorder.

4. *Council, counsel. Council*: an assembly—" the borough council " ; *counsel* : advice—" His father's counsel was wise." *Counsel* can also mean a barrister.

5. *Delusion, illusion, hallucination. Delusion* : mental deception—" He suffers from the delusion that all people respect him." *Illusion* : a deception practised upon the senses—"A mirage is an optical illusion." *Hallucination* : a deception of the senses caused by an unhealthy mind— " In his delirium he suffered from the hallucination that he was drowning."

6. *Discover, invent.* We discover something that was already existent—" Columbus discovered America " ; when we invent something we introduce something hitherto unknown—" Bell invented the telephone."

7. *Economic, economical.* The first means " pertaining

to economics," *e.g. an economic depression,* the second "frugal, cheap "—*an economical method of lighting the house.*

8. *Effect, affect. Effect* : to accomplish—" This design was easily effected "; *affect* : to influence—" He was affected by the heat."

9. *Effective, efficient.* An *effective* machine is one which gives the required effect; an *efficient* machine achieves its purpose with the minimum waste.

10. *Emigrate, immigrate. Emigrate*—to leave a country. *Immigrate*—to enter a country.

11. *Expect, suspect. Expect* : look forward to in the future—" I expect he *will* come." *Suspect* : to have an idea that something is happening or has happened—" I suspect he *has* come." " *Suspect* " is generally used to denote suspicion.

12. *Historic, historical.* We say : " an historic castle," *i.e.,* a castle interesting historically; " an historical novel " means a novel dealing with history.

13. *Imaginary, imaginative. Imaginary* is something not real, *e.g.* "An imaginary line." *Imaginative* : filled with imagination, *e.g.* " He was an imaginative child."

14. *Ingenuous, ingenious. Ingenuous* : frank, lacking in guile—" She has an ingenuous face." *Ingenious* : clever—" an ingenious person."

15. *Insuperable, invincible. Insuperable* means " that which cannot be overcome "; *invincible* " that which cannot be conquered." We speak of an " insuperable difficulty," but " an invincible army."

16. *Lonely, solitary.* Both these words mean alone, without companion; but there is a certain difference of usage. Thus we should say " The ship was wrecked off a lonely coast," not " a solitary coast "; but " There was only a solitary ship in sight."

17. *Luxuriant, luxurious.* *Luxuriant* means "abundant "—usually applied to plants, *e.g.* " the luxuriant vegetation of the tropics "; *luxurious* means " conducive to, or furnished with, luxury," as " a luxurious suite of rooms."

18. *Nationalism, nationalisation.* *Nationalism* denotes " a feeling for and pride in nationality "; *nationalisation,* "the act of bringing trades, industries, etc., under the control of the State," *e.g.* " the nationalisation of the coal mines." " Italian nationalism has become much stronger under Mussolini."

19. *Noted, notorious.* *Noted* means well known or celebrated, *e.g.* " a noted statesman." *Notorious* means well known for one's misdeeds, *e.g.,* " Smith was a notorious murderer."

20. *Possible, probable.* *Possible* means " that which may happen "; *probable,* "that which is likely to happen."

21. *Presumptuous, presumptive.* *Presumptuous* means " excessively bold," while *presumptive* also has the sense of based on probable evidence, *e.g.* " a presumptive opinion," " a presumptuous fellow."

22. *Principle, principal.* " The principle of electromagnetic waves," but " the principal of a school." *Principle*—the law or cause underlying any action; *principal*—chief.

23. *Second, secondary.* The former is the ordinal numeral—"that next to the first "; the latter has also the sense of being subordinate to that which is primary. " He was the second man here." " This is not the chief cause, it is of merely secondary importance."

24. *Temporal, temporary.* *Temporal* has the sense of secular, that which is opposed to the spiritual or the ecclesiastical, as for example " the temporal power of the

Pope "; *temporary* means just " transient, not lasting,"
as " temporary offices, a temporary master, etc."

The following is a list of pairs of words easily confused.
Make sure that you grasp the difference between each
by referring to a good dictionary and noting the exact
meanings given.

artificial, artistic, artful.   inmate, innate.
ascertain, discover.   interpellate, interpolate.
attempt, endeavour.   lay, lie.
beastly, bestial.   marine, maritime.
canvas, canvass.   mendacity, mendicity.
continual, continuous.   mystic, mysterious.
comprehend, apprehend.   orient, oriental.
create, generate.   opponent, enemy.
credible, credulous.   person, personage.
cynic, sceptic.   practice, practise.
deceased, diseased.   prophecy, prophesy.
dependant, dependent.   raise, rise.
dominate, domineer.   refectory, refractory.
doubtful, dubious.   restoration, resurrection.
elicit, illicit.   rural, rustic.
eminent, imminent.   sensuous, sensual.
fashion, manner, way.   sentiment, sentimentality.
healthy, salubrious.   stationary, stationery.
illegal, illegitimate.   tractable, tractile.

The following is a short list of uncommon words which
should be looked up in a dictionary and their exact meanings
noted.

Assonance compared with resonance.
Hegemony.   Polity.
Historicity.   Protocol.
Impercipient.   Nescience.
Perspicuous.   Perspicacious.

QUESTIONS

1. Write sentences to illustrate the differences in meaning between the following pairs of words :

> (a) salutary, salubrious.
>
> (b) beneficent, beneficial.
>
> (c) imply, infer.
>
> (d) exotic, exoteric.
>
> (e) egregious, gregarious.
>
> (f) mendacity, mendicity.
>
> (g) literate, literal.
>
> (h) genius, genus.
>
> (i) valuable, invaluable.
>
> (j) innate, inmate.
>
> (k) specie, species.
>
> (l) impercipient, imperceptible.
>
> (m) euphemism, euphuism.
>
> (n) tolerable, tolerant.
>
> (o) corruptible, corrosive.

2. Explain and illustrate the use of the following words :

Disparity, genesis, redundance, plutocrat, dispensation, nucleus, neologism, tally, distrain, redolent, accord, tractable, bissextile, tractility, hyperbole, subrogation, germane, demesne.

3. Indicate and correct any errors in the use of words in the following sentences :

> (a) Electricity is a comparatively modern invention.
>
> (b) This land is not tractable and therefore useless for agriculture.
>
> (c) You shall comprehend all vagrant men.
>
> (d) Comparisons are odorous.
>
> (e) The conservatory was full of erotic plants.

(*f*) I expect he heard the news before we did.

(*g*) We passed over the historical bridge of Stirling.

(*h*) He is a close acquaintance of mine.

(*i*) Drunkenness was considered the most venal of all peccadilloes.

CHAPTER XIII

THE letter is probably the commonest form of composition. People who never have occasion to compose an essay frequently find themselves called upon to write letters to friends and others. In fact, the writing of a letter is such an everyday affair with most of us that little thought is given to the method to be employed. Yet there is an art in letter writing, as in other forms of composition. In the past, when life was more leisurely, great pains were taken in the writing of letters, whereas, to-day, the tendency is to dispose of them in the shortest possible time. The letters of Lamb, Horace Walpole, and others have become classics, and certainly show the heights which can be reached in the art.

We will, in the first place, consider the parts into which a letter may be divided, and then proceed with the points peculiar to (*a*) personal, and (*b*) business letters.

Parts of a Letter : A complete letter may be divided into the following parts :

1. The address of the sender.
2. The date. This appears immediately below the sender's address.
3. The inside address. This is the name and address of the person to whom the letter is addressed. An inside address is not used in a personal letter.
4. The salutation, viz. the term, such as *Dear Sir*, with which the letter begins.

5. The body matter, viz. the whole subject matter of the letter.

6. The complimentary close—this being the words with which the letter is rounded off.

7. The signature of the writer.

Lay-out of a Letter : A letter, whether of a business or a personal nature, should be laid out properly ; a neat and correct lay-out is pleasing to the eye, whereas an untidy or poor lay-out will have the opposite effect. The following specimen of a properly laid out letter should be studied carefully, particular attention being paid to the different parts as marked.

THE MISCELLANEOUS TRADING CO. LTD.

> 19–27 *Old John Street,*⎫ *Sender's*
> *Birmingham.* ⎭ *Address.*
>
> 21*st September,* 19... *Date.*

Inside Address—Mr. W. G. Lewis,
> 5 *New Walk,*
> *Manchester.*

Salutation—DEAR SIR,

> *Body—*

I have to inform you that we have decided to appoint you as our district representative for Birmingham.

The appointment will date from Monday next, the 26th September, and will be subject to the following terms and conditions :

1. Salary to be at the rate of £240 per annum.
2. All approved expenses to be paid by the Company.
3. Commission of $3\frac{3}{4}\%$ on all sales over £5,000 per year.
4. Salary and expenses to be paid monthly, and commission yearly.
5. Three months' notice on either side.

We shall require you to devote your whole time and energies to your position; to respect any secret or confidential information relating to the Company's business which may come into your possession; to furnish such particulars and accounts with regard to orders, etc. as may be required, and to work generally under the direction of the Sales Superintendent.

The foregoing will be embodied in a service agreement to be executed before you begin your duties.

You will be expected to report at these offices on Monday next, the 26th September, for further instructions.

Complimentary close— Yours truly,

Signature— THE MISCELLANEOUS TRADING Co. LTD.

I. WRIGHT.

Secretary.

Personal Letters. The general tone of a friendly letter should be intimate and free, and characterised by the absence of formal and stilted language. At the same time, the general rules of grammar and construction must be regarded. Bad grammar, or slipshod construction, is no more permissible in a letter than it is in any other form of composition.

Although the style must be lively, slang should be avoided. In order to maintain interest, an abundance of interesting detail should be included. It is really amazing how, with a little care in construction, the most commonplace happenings can be endowed with a very real interest.

The letter must not be one-sided; references to the doings, state of health and suggestions made by the recipient can be relied upon to please him much more than would a letter in which these are not mentioned.

Thus, in a letter to a friend describing a day by the

sea, we could make a few comparisons between a previous day spent with him either by the sea or elsewhere. It is perhaps needless to say that in these comparisons an even balance should be maintained, neither being unduly praised at the expense of the other.

Points to be Avoided in Writing Personal Letters :

1. Do not boast or say anything which is likely to hurt the feelings of the receiver.

2. Do not use *I* excessively.

3. Avoid downright slang. Such contractions as *can't, don't,* etc., may be employed where they fit in with the general tone of the letter.

4. Suit the language to your correspondent. A letter to an intelligent adult would require to be written in a totally different manner from one to a small child. In the latter case the aim of the writer should be to use the simplest language, and to keep the sentences as short as possible.

5. Do not use a postscript unless it conveys a message to be delivered to a third party which could not be conveniently included in the body of the letter.

6. Avoid underlining, unless the word underlined is to be read as italicised.

7. Do not close with a crude excuse such as : *I must rush for the post ; Mother is calling me,* or *I have run out of ink.* The letter should always end on a note of interest or suspense, e.g., *I have much more to tell you when we meet ; I wonder if John likes his job as much as he says he does ; What do you think of my idea.* In other words, the recipient should be given something to think about after he has finished reading the letter.

Salutation and Close. There should be a definite relationship between these—the tone of the salutation harmonising with that of the close. In a private letter the degree of friendship between the sender and the recipient will indicate the warmth to be used in the salutation and close. The greater the friendship, the warmer should these be. The general rules in writing personal letters may be summarised as follows :—

1. *A casual acquaintance.* Begin : *Dear Mr.* (Mrs. Miss) *Smith ;* conclude *Yours truly* or *Yours Sincerely.*

2. *Parents and other relations.* Begin : *Dear Mother* (Uncle George; Cousin; Cousin Jim). *My* may be added before *Dear.* In the case of cousins, brothers and sisters and aunts or uncles of about the same age as the writer, the degree of relationship is often omitted, e.g. *My dear Sydney.* Letters to relations may be concluded *Your affectionate daughter* (Uncle, Cousin, etc.).

3. *Very intimate friends.* Begin : *My dear James,* (Dorothy, etc.) Conclude with : *Your affectionate friend.* Intimate men friends usually address each other as, e.g. *My dear Robinson* and conclude *Yours very sincerely.*

The following is a specimen of a personal letter written by Charles Lamb. Unfortunately, owing to lack of space, it has been abridged, but the delightful whole may be read in the *Essays of Elia.*

My Dear F.—When I think how welcome the sight of a letter from the world where you were born must be to you in that strange one to which you have been transplanted, I feel some compunctious visitings at my long silence. But, indeed, it is no easy effort to set about a correspondence at our distance. The weary world of waters between us oppresses the imagination. It is difficult to conceive how a scrawl of mine should ever stretch across it. It is a sort of presumption to expect that one's thoughts should live so far. It is like writing for posterity ; and reminds me of one of Mrs. Rowe's superscriptions, " Alcander to Strephon in the shades." Cowley's Post-Angel is no more than would be expedient in such an intercourse. One drops a packet at

Lombard Street, and in twenty-four hours a friend in Cumberland gets it as fresh as if it came in ice. It is only like whispering through a long trumpet. But suppose a tube let down from the moon, with yourself at one end, and *the man* at the other; it would be some balk to the spirit of conversation, if you knew that the dialogue exchanged with that interesting theosophist would take two or three revolutions of a higher luminary in its passage. Yet for aught I know, you may be some parasangs nigher that primitive idea—Plato's man—than we in England here have the honour to reckon ourselves.

Epistolary matter usually compriseth three topics— news, sentiment, and puns. In the latter, I include all non-serious subjects; or subjects serious in themselves, but treated after my fashion, non-seriously. And first, for news. In them the most desirable circumstances, I suppose, is that they shall be true. But what security can I have that what I now send you for truth shall not, before you get it, unaccountably turn into a lie? For instance, our mutual friend P. is at this present writing—my Now—in good health, and enjoys a fair share of worldly reputation. You are glad to hear it. This is natural and friendly. But at this present reading—your Now—he may possibly be in the Bench, or going to be hanged, which in reason ought to abate something of your transport (i.e., at hearing he was well, etc.), or at least considerably to modify it. I am going to the play this evening to have a laugh with Munden You have no theatre, I think you told me, in your land. You naturally lick your lips, and envy me my felicity. Think but a moment, and you will correct the hateful emotion. Why is it Sunday morning with you, and 1823? This confusion of tenses, this grand solecism of two presents, is in a degree common to all postage. But if I sent you word to Bath or Devizes, that I was expecting the aforesaid treat this evening, though at the moment you received the intelligence, my full feast of fun would be over, yet there would be for a day or two after, as you would well know, a smack, a relish left upon my mental palate, which would give rational encouragement for you to foster a portion at least of the disagreeable passion which it was in part my

intention to produce. But ten months hence, your envy
or your sympathy would be as useless as a passion spent
upon the dead.

Then as to sentiment. It fares little better with that.
This kind of dish, above all, requires to be served up hot;
or sent off in water-plates, that your friend may have it
almost as warm as yourself. If it have time to cool, it is
the most tasteless of all cold meats. I have often smiled
at a conceit of the late Lord C. It seems that travelling
somewhere about Geneva, he came to some pretty green
spot, or nook, where a willow, or something hung so fan-
tastically and invitingly over a stream—was it?—or a
rock?—no matter—but the stillness and the repose, after a
weary journey 'tis likely, in a languid moment of his Lordship's hot restless life, so took his fancy that he could
imagine no place so proper, in the event of his death, to
lay his bones in. This was all very natural and excusable
as a sentiment, and shows his character in a very pleasing
light. But when from a passing sentiment it came to be
an act; and when, by a positive testamentary disposal, his
remains were actually carried all that way from England;
who was there, some desperate sentimentalists excepted,
that did not ask the question, Why could not his Lordship
have found a spot as solitary, a nook as romantic, a tree as
green and pendent, with a stream as emblematic to his
purpose, in Surrey, in Dorset, or in Devon?

Lastly, as to the agreeable levities, which though contempt-
ible in bulk, are the twinkling corpuscula which should
irradiate a right friendly epistle—your puns and small jests
are, I apprehend, extremely circumscribed in their sphere
of action. They are so far from a capacity of being packed
up and sent beyond sea, they will scarce endure to be
transported by hand from this room to the next. A pun
hath a hearty kind of present ear-kissing smack with it:
you can no more transmit it in its pristine flavour, than you
can send a kiss. Have you not tried in some instances to
palm off a yesterday's pun upon a gentleman, and has it
answered? Not but it was new to his hearing, but it did
not seem to come new from you. It did not hitch in. It
was like picking up at a village ale-house a two-days'-old

newspaper. You have not seen it before, but you resent
the stale thing as an affront. This sort of merchandise
above all requires a quick return. A pun, and its recognitory
laugh, must be co-instantaneous.

I am insensibly chatting to you as familiarly as when
we used to exchange good-morrows out of our old con-
tiguous windows, in pump-famed Hare Court in the Temple.
Why did you ever leave that quiet corner? Why did
I? With its complement of four poor elms, from whose
smoked-dyed barks, the theme of jesting ruralists, I picked
my first lady-birds! My heart is as dry as that spring
sometimes proves in a thirsty August, when I revert to the
space that is between us; a length of passage enough to
render obsolete the phrases of our English letters before
they can reach you. But while I talk, I think you hear me.
Come back, before I am grown into a very old man, so as
you shall hardly know me. Come, before Bridget walks
on crutches. Girls whom you left children have become
sage matrons while you are tarrying there. The blooming
Miss W——r (you remember Sally W——r) called upon
us yesterday, an aged crone. Folks, whom you knew, die off
every year. Formerly, I thought that death was wearing
out—I stood ramparted about with so many healthy
friends. The departure of J. W., two springs back, corrected
my delusion. Since then the old divorcer has been busy.
If you do not make haste to return, there will be little left
to greet you, of me, or mine.

An Example of a Simpler Form of Private Letter :

In this example we have taken the kind of letter which
a business man might write to a friend combining, as it
were, business with pleasure.

> Old Oak House,
> Westward Avenue,
> Woking.
> 17th Feb., 19...

My dear James,

I was glad to hear from you that young Brown
has matriculated, and, of course, remember my promise
to get him a start in business. Unfortunately, my own

P

office is rather overstaffed at the moment, but I think I can persuade Smithers to take him for a few months, after which I should be able to find room for him myself. I will let you know as soon as I am able to arrange an opening for Brown.

I saw your friend Howard the other day, and he enquired after your welfare. He is still as cheerful and incorrigible as ever; and as popular.

If you are able to come up to town for a day or two I would like you to do so. Grace will be delighted to see you again, and there is also the matter of the securities which you propose selling. I would like to have a chat with you concerning these before you do anything in the matter.

Kind regards to Mrs. J.

Yours very sincerely,

HENRY.

Business Letters : Although this book is not meant to be a treatise on business letters, it is felt that a few of the rules to be observed and the pitfalls to be avoided may be usefully given.

1. The letter must be written in good English. It is a mistaken impression amongst many that a business letter must be written in a special kind of English. This probably accounts for the appearance of such phrases as : *Re yours of the* 16*th ult ; Yours of even date to hand*, etc. There is no justification whatever for employing these terms, and a good correspondent will avoid them.

2. *Clarity and completeness.* The recipient must not be left in any doubt as to exactly what is meant, nor must any point be overlooked. Incompleteness usually arises through the omission to answer a question raised in the letter to which one is replying.

3. *Brevity.* This means that the matter must be disposed of as shortly as possible, but the rules of clarity and completeness must be observed.

4. *Courtesy.* Even where the intended recipient has been foolish or abusive, a courteous reply should be given. Servility, however, which must be distinguished from courtesy, must never be practised.

Types of Business Letters

Business letters may be divided broadly into three different types :

1. *Those of a routine nature,* such as acknowledgment of orders, covering letters for remittances and documents, etc.

2. *Those requiring tactful answers.* A letter such as this would be needed, *e.g.* where an influential customer requires an employee to be reprimanded, although the latter has only done his duty. The customer must not be offended, and, at the same time, the reprimand cannot be carried out. Such letters require a great amount of thought and tact before they can be properly answered.

3. *Those requiring technical or legal knowledge,* as, *e.g.*, a letter from the secretary of a company to a shareholder who wants the company to buy back his shares, or from an engineer concerning technical points in the running of machinery.

The first type of letter is easy, and a knowledge of the lay-out of a letter plus good composition are all that are necessary. The second can only be dealt with by a practised and experienced correspondent. The third type requires technical qualifications. The difficulties in connection with business letters will be appreciated when it is stated that many of them come within both categories 2 and 3.

QUESTIONS

Private Letters :

1. Describing to a friend a sea cruise.
2. Describing a visit to either a museum or a factory.
3. Explaining to a small child the main objects of education.
4. Accepting an invitation to spend a holiday with a friend.
5. Inviting a friend to spend a holiday with yourself.
6. Reply letters to 4. and 5.
7. Giving an account of a visit to a foreign country.
8. To a town dweller giving a description of country life.
9. Describing a picture or play which you have recently seen.

Business Letters :

1. Applying for a situation as junior clerk.
2. Requiring particulars of cloths (from a retailer to a manufacturer).
3. Enclosing a catalogue and offering for sale the goods described therein.
4. Accepting an offer for the sale of goods.
5. Complaining of defects in goods purchased.
6. A circular stating that you have recently opened up business in the district.

CHAPTER XIV

IN a number of the minor Civil Service examinations candidates are required to make a copy of a written manuscript. The original may be quite straightforward, or it may contain alterations, erasures and insets, but, in either case, the answer should be given as a fair copy of the original, with any spelling mistakes corrected.

In some cases the writing in the original is almost illegible, but it is always possible to supply the correct words by an intelligent following of the sense of the passage.

The copying of manuscripts is not a subject in which actual instruction can be given; facility will come with practice. The usual difficulty encountered is to find sufficient time to make a fair copy of the original in the time allowed. A few hints in this connection should be enough to ensure that the best possible use is made of the available time.

1. Read through the original carefully, pencilling over any illegible words, the words you think they are intended to represent.

2. See that your pencilled words under 1 fit in with the sense of the passage. If there are possible alternatives and it appears impossible to decide which to use, take the one that appears to be most in keeping with the general sense and tone of the original.

3. Make your fair copy writing both quickly and legibly. Take particular care to see that any additions and alterations are included in the appropriate place.

I once sent a few of my short stories to a publisher who advertised for new writers. I had a letter from him by return of post. "These," he wrote, "are capital. Fresh, original, capital." And he asked me to put down the sum of £95 "towards the cost of publishing a book." He enclosed booklet called "Tips to Authors" which told you that your first task was to obtain paper to write on, unless you preferred a copy book, and that you could write either in ink or pencil. Stories, you were wisely informed, could be either short or long. And so on. In conclusion, the writer of the booklet asked permission to be allowed to wish you luck. I declined, however, to provide the £95 whereupon the publisher suddenly lost all interest in the freshness and originality of my stories.

222

EXAMPLES

Two examples are given on pp. 222 and 224 the first being merely a rather illegibly written passage, and the second containing alterations, etc.

Fair Copy.

I once sent a few of my short stories to a publisher who advertised for new writers. I had a letter from him by return of post. " These," he wrote, " are capital. Fresh, original, capital." And he asked me to put down the sum of £95 " towards the cost of publishing a book." He enclosed a booklet called " Tips to Authors," which told you that your first task was to obtain paper to write on, unless you preferred a copy-book, and that you could write either in ink or pencil. Stories, you were wisely informed, could be written either short or long. And so on. In conclusion, the writer of the booklet asked per-mission to be allowed to wish you luck. I declined, however, to provide the £95, whereupon the publisher suddenly lost all interest in the freshness and originality of my stories!

Notes

The seventh word might be almost anything, but the sense of the passage clearly indicates that *my* is the correct word. The same remarks apply to the words *sum* (sixth line down), and others which need not be enumerated here.

You and *your* (ninth line down) could easily be confused, but here again the sense of the passage will keep us right.

Fair Copy of MS. on page 224.

My friend John, who was always up to date in dress, was most pleased with himself several years ago when he bought his first plus-four suit. He secured an excellent pair of sporting stockings and thought himself in the height of fashion because from the top of the left stocking who was always up to date in dress,

several My friend John was most pleased with himself about years ago when he bought an excellent new his first plus-four suit He secured some sporting stockings and thought himself he was in the height of fashion because

What appeared to be a tassel of wool was suspended from the top of the left stocking He was at first tassel puzzled because no loop could was to be found on the right other stocking but he decided that this was quite covered in order;

But happening then to call again at the hosier he mentioned the tassel loop and said how that he was pleased he was with the new notion. Suppressing with difficulty his mirth the hosier informed John that the tassel loop was not a wool decoration at all, but was simply wool to be used when darning the stocking Since that day John hasn't been seen in plus-fours.

And so for a few days he enjoyed the splendour of his suit.

was suspended what appeared to be a tassel of wool. He was puzzled because no tassel was to be found on the right stocking, but he decided that this was quite in order; and so for a few days he enjoyed the splendour of his suit. But happening then to call at the hosier's again, he mentioned the tassel and said how pleased he was with the new notion. Suppressing his mirth with difficulty, the hosier informed John that the tassel was not a decoration at all, but was simply wool to be used when darning the stockings. Since that day John hasn't been seen in plus fours.

Notes: The fair copy disposes of most of the difficulties arising in the original, although there is still one point which calls for special mention. This is the word *stocking* in the inset to the third line from the bottom. It is impossible to see whether the blob is meant for an *s* or a full stop, but as the wool is obviously intended for the mending of both stockings we have assumed that the plural was meant. There is further justification for this assumption in that the word *wool* appears to be followed by a full stop which has not been deleted. In cases where the deciphering is extremely difficult, help may be obtained in comparing letters in the same original. For instance, if we are in doubt as to whether a letter is an *e* or an *i*, we can compare it with the same formation in some other word in which there is no doubt as to which it is. Similarly with word endings. A number of persons do not complete their *r's*, which may cause confusion as to whether *-r* in a given word is, *e.g.*, *you* or *your*. A comparison of the incomplete letter with an *r* as formed in another word, preferably at the end, will do much to remove any doubt. In fact, in all cases of extreme doubt a careful comparison of the doubtful letters with others where there is no doubt, should ensure that all illegible words are correctly deciphered.

Phonetic Spelling

In a few of the Civil Service examinations a passage is written phonetically, and candidates are required to copy it out in orthodox spelling. A key to sound values is given, and the exercise should present no difficulty to those who are able to spell reasonably well, and also able to exercise common sense in the use of the key.

In order to show exactly what is required, an example is given below :

Orthography

Time allowed, half-an-hour.

Write out the following passage in the customary spelling. The values of the symbol are shown below in the Key to sound Values.

thi fashun ov rœd-maikiŋ in this kuntri iz tu folœ thi rœman prinsipl ov maiki rœdz az strait az posibl. this iz unfortyunait. thi rœmanz wer ailienz an koŋkerorz and thair rœdz wer maid for militari purposiz, tu privent eni los o tiem in mœviŋ about thi kuntri and tu avoid eni posibiliti ov surpriez an ambush thi rœman rœdz—thœez dierekt unbendiŋ lienz—performd a defini fuŋkshun for thi rœman armiz but nouadaiz we ned not tret thi iŋglis kuntrisied sœ krœeli. meni ov us diplœr thi hycoj loŋ kutiŋz which ar ofe maid in order tu taik of thre. fœr, or fiev fet from thi krests ov hilz sœ tha automœbelz, insted ov gœiŋ kwikli, kan gœ veri kwikli. sum ov us ar not a aul konvinst that sped iz a paiŋ propozishun a chienaman woz wuns tœl that bie a nyœ form ov transport he wud be aibl tu rech a sertin plais te minits kwiker than he utherwiez kud. he riplied : "yœ get ten minits ; who dœ yœ dœ with them ?" yœ kan frekwentli spend ten minits on thi rœ kwiet az profitabli az at thi destinaishun. thi imprœvment ov rœdz shud no distroi thair nachural chaarm or thi bycoti ov thi kuntri.

KEY TO SOUND VALUES.

a	is pronounced as in	bat.	ou	is pronounced as in	south (south).	
e	,,	yes.	g	,,	get.	
i	,,	pit.	s	,,	sister.	
o	.	pot.	y	,,	yet.	
u	,,	but.	ch	,,	church (church)	
ʊ	,,	put (put).	sh	,,	shut (shut).	
aɹ	,,	ask (aask).	wh	,,	when (when).	
aɪ	,,	maid (maid).	zh	has the value of si in fusion (fyœzhun)		
aʊ	,,	haul (haul).	th	is pronounced as in thin (thin).		
eə	.	keel (keel).	th	,,	this (this).	
ie	,,	pie (pie).	ŋ	,,	long (loŋ).	
œ	,,	toe (tœ).	c q x are not used ; other letters no			
ɷ	,,	boot (bœt).	shown have their customary sounds.			

Passage Written out in Correct Spelling.

The fashion of road-making in this country is to follow the Roman principle of making roads as straight as possible. This is unfortunate. The Romans were aliens and conquerors and their roads were made for military purposes, to prevent any loss of time in moving about the country and to avoid any possibility of surprise and ambush. The Roman roads—those direct unbending lines—performed a definite function for the Roman armies. But nowadays we need not treat the English countryside so cruelly. Many of us deplore the huge long cuttings which are often made in order to take off three, four or five feet from the crests of hills so that automobiles, instead of going quickly, can go very quickly. Some of us are not at all convinced that speed is a paying proposition. A Chinaman was once told that by a new form of transport he would be able to reach a certain place ten minutes quicker than he otherwise could. He replied : " You get ten minutes; what do you do with them ? " You can frequently spend ten minutes on the road quite as profitably as at the destination. The improvement of roads should not destroy their natural charm or the beauty of the country.

Note : It will be seen that capital letters are put in where necessary, and this is what is required.

QUESTIONS

Make a fair copy of each of the following manuscripts, correcting the spelling where necessary.

Dear S——

I have been thinking a great deal lately
about earning a little money for myself and at last
I have had an inspiration. I have decided
to go in for the prize competition in the Westminster
Gazette. It seems they offer quite good prizes
every week, and Aunt Mary once knew a girl
who had earned three guineas as a prize and
who seemed quite confident she could earn much
more if she tried. The competition for next
week is really quite easy. You have to write
a poem of four lines, the first two lines of which
end with the words 'editor' and 'coastguard'
Somehow I haven't got on far yet, but I
am sure it will come all right in the end.
If you think of any words that rhyme with
'editor', do let me know before Thursday.

Editors of newspapers receive many strange letters from odd people with bees in their bonnets but perhaps the strangest letter ever opened in a newspaper office was one which read as follows " I like your paper very much, dear Editor, and am very pleased with the articles which you have published on many interesting & instructive topics. But there is one subject with which you do not seem to have dealt at all. I think the subject is very important indeed and it is this — why are not coffins made with hinged lids so that, if necessary, they could be opened from inside ? I hope you will see your way to give as much publicity as possible to this important matter. Public opinion must be aroused against the undertakers."!

My father, having lost almost all his money, devised a system of making a fortune at roulette. My father & I spent many weeks at home testing the system on a roulette which I bought at a big store & the initial results were favourable. Then I went to Monte Carlo. I was a bit put out as I sat down at the table, by a woman who lost 100 francs and began to cry softly. At the end of three hours I found myself the winner of five francs. In the afternoon I was let down at the start. Our "system" did not provide for losing at the start, and I could not retrieve my loss. Indeed, the next morning further losses were, most unfairly, I thought, added to those of the day before. So I left for home immediately. In the train two English ladies told me you could make a steady income at roulette if you were steady & knew when to stop, etc. "Yes," I said gloomily, "Yes".

Mr. Jones had hardly gone twenty yards when his eye was attracted by a small object lying in the thick grass. He stooped to pick it up & uttered an exclamation of delight. It was a tiny model of a parrot, quaintly wrought in bronze — not more than two & a half inches high, including the pedestal on which it stood. A hole had been made through the eyes and a strand of silken thread yet remained to shew, by its frayed ends, how the treasure had been lost. Mr. Jones was charmed; it was such a dear little parrot. He was a simple man — small things gave him pleasure; and this small thing pleased him very much. The better to examine his find, he seated himself on a clean white post & proceeded to polish the little parrot with his handkerchief.

CHAPTER XV

In certain examinations, candidates are given some statistical data and required to write a composition on the facts as disclosed. The composition required may take the form either of an essay or, as is more usual, of a newspaper article.

What is required in this type of exercise is a reproduction of the information conveyed by the general trend of the figures; a suggested explanation of the facts and the drawing of attention to any significant variations from the general trend or surprising features.

A composition of this type calls for common sense, imagination, a sound general knowledge and last, but not least, skill in composition. As a rule common sense and imagination will enable us to dig out the facts, while the explanation must be given with the aid of our general knowledge. In this connection it may be noted that the statistics given are almost invariably of a general and not a specialised nature.

The general principles of essay writing will, of course, apply with equal force to this type of composition; in fact, it may be said that such a composition is little else than an essay, the facts for which are given. Figures tend to be dull, and unless we are very careful the interpretation of them will be dull also. This is a fault which must be avoided, every endeavour being made to make the data as lively and interesting as possible. The result should

232

never be a mere representation of the figures in word form.

The steps to be taken in this form of composition are :

1. Jot down in note form the main facts which the figures convey.

2. Note any inferences which may be drawn.

3. Proceed to write the complete composition from the information contained in your notes.

In making these notes the figures given must be examined very carefully. A general trend will probably be disclosed. If it is not, the fact should be noted for inclusion in the answer. A little thought must be given to the significance of the trend—the changes in social or physical conditions indicated—and the reasons for them. Any exceptions or startling facts disclosed should next be noted and an endeavour made to find the causes.

We must, when suggesting explanations, make sure that they are reasonable. If the reason for a certain change is not obvious, it may usually be suggested with the aid of a little imagination, but at the same time imagination must not be allowed to stray from the realms of probability.

It is worth emphasising that the composition must not be thrown together in confusion. Some orderly arrangement is essential. As a rule, the facts can be arranged chronologically. If they cannot, they should be dealt with group by group.

Example 1 :

We will first take a simple case of a few figures, and decide what facts they suggest, and then in Example II proceed to frame a complete answer to a question on the lines of examination requirements.

Q

STREET ACCIDENTS (LONDON)

Time.	Age.		
	7–14.	14–60.	over 60.
Before 9 a.m.	124	76	66
9 a.m. to 12 noon . .	42	97	85
12 noon to 2 p.m. . .	146	108	53
2 p.m. to 4 p.m. . .	73	80	128
4 p.m. to 7 p.m. . .	160	126	49
After 7 p.m.	86	228	42

The facts disclosed by this information may be tabulated as follows :

1. Accidents are heaviest amongst school children after school hours are over. This suggests the desirability of providing some alternative to their playing in the streets.

2. Accidents amongst school children are also heavy during the times when they are going to or returning from school. Drivers of motors and other vehicles should be especially careful during these hours, particularly in the vicinity of schools.

3. The greatest number of accidents occurs after 7 p.m. The number amongst those aged 14–60, who may be regarded as reasonably careful individuals, is especially heavy at these times, thus indicating that the roads are not as safe in the evening as they are during the day. This may be due to the fact that night driving is more dangerous than day driving. Before arriving at a definite conclusion on this point we should need to know whether the figures for this time were heavier in winter than in summer.

4. Accidents amongst those over 60 are heaviest between 2 p.m. and 4 p.m. This is probably natural since these are the hours when the greatest number of elderly persons may be assumed to be out walking. This

fact suggests that such persons should be especially careful when crossing the roads, particularly as they may be deaf or short-sighted.

5. The general inference is that street accidents in London are far too numerous. Some suggestions as to how they might be reduced could be noted for inclusion.

Example II :

State in the form of an interesting article the facts conveyed by the following figures and the inferences you would draw from them.

BIRTH AND DEATH RATES FOR ENGLAND AND WALES

Year.	Births per 1,000 of population.	Deaths per 1,000 of population.	Deaths of infants under 1 year per 1,000 of population.
1856	34·1	22·2	154
1880	34·2	20·5	153
1890	30·2	19·5	151
1900	28·7	18·2	154
1910	25·1	13·5	105
1915	21·9	15·7	110
1917	17·8	14·2	96
1919	18·5	13·7	89
1921	22·4	12·1	82
1923	19·7	11·6	70
1925	18·3	12·2	75
1926	17·8	11·6	70

London.

1925	18·0	11·7	67
1926	17·1	11·6	64

Great Towns including London.

1925	18·8	12·2	79
1926	18·2	11·6	73

Smaller Towns.

1925	18·3	11·2	74
1926	17·6	10·6	67

The Narrative

Much is heard of the yearly fall in the birth rate, but little of the compensating fall in death rate. Although there has been a steady decline in the birth rate since 1850, the death rate has declined in practically the same proportion, both being in 1926 roughly half of what they were in 1850. Moreover, the fall in the birth rate is not entirely to be lamented. If the death rate had been halved with no corresponding fall in the birth rate, the country would soon have become overcrowded. Indeed if the population had continued to increase at the rate for 1880, when there was the largest recorded excess of births over deaths, saturation point would soon have been reached, to say nothing of the limit of employment, which has apparently been passed already. Thus the falling birth rate is by no means an unmixed evil, while the falling death rate is a pure blessing.

On the other hand, fewer births mean fewer workers, and this fact is lamented by economists who more or less rightly maintain that an increased supply is met by an increased demand.

The birth rate was very high from 1850 to 1880, reaching its peak in the latter year. These were the years of comfortable Victorian prosperity, when large families were in vogue, and could be easily supported. From this point the birth rate began gradually to decrease; the limit of prosperity had been reached; the country could not continue for long to support such an abnormal increase of population. The decline in the number of births was rapid from the outbreak of war in 1914, until in 1917 the rate was only just over half that of 1880. With the end of the war the rate increased again until 1921. But the economic depression following the war made it impossible to provide for a large increase in population. Consequently, the birth rate has fallen continuously between 1921 and 1926.

The decrease in the death rate follows on almost parallel lines. Here again the general trend was interrupted by the Great War, when the hard conditions of life naturally caused an increase in the number of deaths. Apart from this, the fall has been practically uninterrupted. Particularly remarkable is the large decrease between 1900 and 1910. This steady fall reflects great credit upon the increased knowledge and skill of medical practitioners and research workers. Inventions such as the X-rays, increased knowledge of gynecology and the general causes and prevention of disease combined with greater skill in operating have greatly reduced the risk of early deaths.

The increased efficiency of the medical service is shown even more strikingly by the rates for infant mortality. Such deaths have fallen by more than a half from 154 in 1850 to 70 in 1926. It is remarkable that there was no appreciable decrease from 1850 to 1900, but in the following ten years there is the amazing drop of 49 per thousand. The increase of medical knowledge, the provision of clinics and maternity homes and the greater attention to the health of the poor, bore sudden and rich results, and from that time the decrease in infant mortality has been more or less continuous.

Nowadays, conditions seem to be very much the same all over the country, for the rates vary but little. Figures for infant mortality are slightly lower in London than elsewhere; due probably to the fact that the Metropolis enjoys rather better facilities than elsewhere in the form of clinics, etc. On the other hand, the purer air of the smaller

towns seems to be more conducive to health, as their
death rate is below the average. The death rates of the
larger provincial towns mark them as being the least
healthy places. In births London lags behind other
towns, which is rather surprising in view of its rapid
growth.

The falling death rate pays tribute to the advance of
civilisation, on one side at any rate. On the other hand,
the birth rate, in a way, testifies to the great failure of
modern civilisation in the economic sphere, the failure to
reconcile the social and economic structure to modern
conditions. Vital statistics can excuse neither complete
pessimism nor unqualified complacency.

	London.	Paris.	New York.
Approximate population in area covered by returns . .	4½ million	3 million	6 million
Total number of fires other than chimney fires . . .	4,619	3,004	30,994
Causes :			
Stoves, flues, grates and hearths	407	48	877
Hot ashes	116	25	155
Electricity, various causes .	386	321	1,710
Gas	272	49	449
Mineral oil lamps . . .	19	83	46
Candles	132	36	356
Petrol, various causes . .	621	281	5,920
Lights thrown down, matches, smoking, etc. . . .	1,292	237	5,556
Airing bedding, linen, etc. .	49	250	—
Clothing in contact with fire .	27	67	—
Children playing with fire .	77	12	720
Boiling over of fats, grease, etc.	130	61	601
Friction of machinery . .	30	—	119
Spontaneous ignition . .	7	8	259
Explosion	5	87	9
Engine backfiring . . .	—	114	—
Bonfires, brush fires, etc. .	35	—	7,477
Incendiary or suspected . .	1	40	208
Other causes	277	917	2,370
Unknown	129	221	4,319

QUESTIONS

1. The preceding table gives figures relating to the causes of fires in certain cities. Using these figures as a basis, write an article of about 500 words, bringing out the points of greatest interest and commenting on the chief differences between the three cities.

2. With the aid of the data printed below, review the progress of British civil aviation during the years 1919–1926. (The figures take no account of the movements of the Royal Air Force or of private owners : they refer only to British aircraft carrying goods and passengers for hire on regular air-routes.)

	Number of Flights.	Mileage Flown.	Pas-sengers.	Cargo in Tons.	Acci-dents.	Killed.	In-jured.
1919	467	104,000	870	30	2	3	3
1920	2,854	644,000	5,799	137	2	4	2
1921	993	225,000	5,256	19	—	—	—
1922	2,891	717,000	10,393	215	2	2	2
1923	2,559	943,000	15,552	328	3	5	3
1924	2,794	936,000	13,601	543	1	8	—
1925	2,891	862,000	11,193	550	—	—	—
1926	2,879	840,000	16,775	679	—	—	—

3. Below are printed some figures relative to crime in England and Wales during the last two decades. Basing your remarks on these figures, write a leading article for a newspaper, ascribing reasons, where possible, for any notable variations in the figures, and commenting on any points of outstanding interest.

A. Murders in England and Wales (actual figures).

1913	111
1921	90
1930	86
1931	109

B. Indictable offences in England and Wales, per million of the population.

1913	.	.	.	.	.	2,700
1921	.	.	.	.	.	2,700
1929	.	.	.	.	.	3,400
1930	.	.	.	.	.	3,700

C. Indictable offences tried by Juvenile Courts (actual numbers).

1913	.	.	.	.	.	12,900
1921	.	.	.	.	.	10,400
1929	.	.	.	.	.	10,400
1930	.	.	.	.	.	11,100

D. Committals to prison (actual numbers).

	Number committed.	Number committed without option of fine.
1913 . .	167,000	62,000
1921 . .	66,000	(not available)
1930 . .	60,000	26,000

E. Burglaries in the Metropolitan Police District (actual figures).

1913	.	.	.	.	.	3,000
1921	.	.	.	.	.	3,900
1930	.	.	.	.	.	5,700
1931	.	.	.	.	.	8,000

F. " Smash-and-Grab " raids in the same district (average per month).

1925	.	.	.	.	.	11
1929	.	.	.	.	.	19
1930	.	.	.	.	.	20
1931	.	.	.	.	.	16
1932 (first 3 months)	.	.	27

4. The diagram given below shows for the period 1917 to 1929 the variations in the cost of living, and, with regard to agriculture, the variations in the minimum wage, the cost of labour, and the prices of produce. Study the diagram with a view to ascertaining the light which it throws on the position of the farmer and the farm labourer in this country since 1917. Then write as if for a news-

paper an article of not more than 400 words likely to interest the general reader, embodying your observations and inferences and any explanations of the chief variations in the graphs that may occur to you.

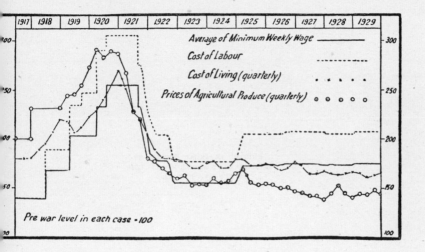

PRINTED IN GREAT BRITAIN BY
RICHARD CLAY AND COMPANY, LTD.,
BUNGAY, SUFFOLK